Vignettes from Heaven, Vol. 2

THE MORE
EXCELLENT WAY

Tracee Anne Loosle

A Divine RE – The More Excellent Way
Vignettes from Heaven, Volume 2
© 2022 Tracee Anne Loosle

All Rights Reserved. No part of this publication may be reproduced, stored in a retrieval system or transmitted in any form or by any means – electronic, mechanical, photocopy, recording or any other – except for brief quotations in printed reviews, without the prior permission of the author.

Scripture quotations marked NASB are taken from the NEW AMERICAN STANDARD BIBLE®, Copyright ©1960,1962,1963,1968, 1971,1972,1973,1975,1977,1995 by The Lockman Foundation. Used by permission.

Scripture quotations marked TPT are from The Passion Translation®. Copyright © 2017, 2018, 2020 by Passion & Fire Ministries, Inc. Used by permission. All rights reserved. ThePassionTranslation.com.

Scripture quotations marked MSG are taken from The Message. Copyright © 1993, 1994, 1995, 1996, 2000, 2001, 2002. Used by permission of NavPress Publishing Group.

Scripture quotations marked AMPC are taken from Amplified Bible, Classic Edition Copyright © 1954, 1958, 1962, 1964, 1965, 1987 by The Lockman Foundation

Scripture quotations marked (KJV) have been taken from the King James Version. Public Domain.

ISBN: 979-8-9858779-0-8

Intrepidheart.org
contact: admin@intrepidheart.org

Printed in the United States of America.
For worldwide distribution.

A Divine Re-

    The More Excellent Way

Journey with the Way, the Truth and the Life.

Jesus Christ is the More Excellent Way.

Written with the One Who is Love to me,
Yeshua my Beloved.

ACKNOWLEDGMENTS

The process of writing is shared with those who take the raw pieces of story and turn it into pages of clarity. I had two gifted women help with this book who I want to honor and thank. Lynnell Ramey proofed the first and last draft. Thank you, Lynnell ,for your excellent contribution. Carol Martinez took the draft, edited it. and put it into the beautiful layout you are holding. Thank you, Carol, for your extraordinary creativity and input. Together the message of hope is woven with chords of love, grace, and glory.

Thank you, Steve Fryer of Steve Fryer Design, for the beautiful cover design.

TABLE OF CONTENTS

1. A Divine RE– ... 13
2. An Epiphany ... 17
3. Wings of Hope ... 19
4. The More Excellent Way ... 23
5. Game Changer ... 25
6. Transcendent Love ... 29
7. Sign of Power ... 33
8. RE-calibrate ... 35
9. Silence Is Still ... 37
10. To Sit and Be ... 41
11. Hoops and Systems ... 43
12. Pariah ... 47
13. The Sin-Bearer ... 49
14. Identity–Genuine–Real ... 53
15. The Measure of Grace ... 55
16. Perfect ... 59
17. Imagine Branding Jesus ... 61
18. Jesus' Blood Speaks ... 65
19. You're Something! Who Are You? ... 67
20. Who Are You? ... 69
21. See What Is Hidden ... 73
22. Upheavals ... Stay Steady...79
23. A Re–Season ... 85
24. Omni Vision ... 87
25. Wisdom Speaks ... 93
26. When Dreams Die ... 97
27. Hope Awakened ... 99
28. Satisfy the Weary ... 101
29. Grief ... 105
30. Transition of the Lord ... 107

A Divine RE- The More Excellent Way

31.	Jesus, You're Enough ... 111	
32.	Renew Your Mind ... 113	
33.	Your Mouth – A Womb or a Tomb? ... 115	
34.	RE-turn ... 119	
35.	Lost in the Race ... 121	
36.	Leaning ... 125	
37.	Unravel the Motives ... 127	
38.	Re-Turn to Son-Ship ... 129	
39.	Celebrated, not Tolerated: Truth or Fairy Tale? ... 133	
40.	Turning Point ... 139	
41.	Sunday of All Sundays ... 145	
42.	Rhythms of Grace ... 147	
43.	In-Between ... 149	
44.	The Silent Pause ... 151	
45.	The Lessons of Dolphins ... 153	
46.	Behold Deliverance ... 155	
47.	See Three ... 161	
48.	Brokenness and Beauty ... 165	
49.	Broken and Poured Out ... 169	
50.	Pools of Bethesda ... 173	
51.	Stand ... 179	
52.	Pioneer ... 181	
53.	Settle—Absolutely Not! ... 183	
54.	Established to Flourish ... 185	
55.	Divine Purpose in Upheaval ... 191	
56.	Go Through ... 195	
57.	Awakened to Truth ... 199	
58.	Move Forward ... 203	
59.	Re-Generation ... 209	
60.	Power of Love ... 213	
61.	The "It Is Finished" Posture ... 215	
62.	Re-Boot ... 219	
63.	A Crown ... 223	

The More Excellent Way

In Christ—
   The past is gone,
To be remembered
   No more.

Failures become
   Stepping stones
Upon the highway of grace.

Climbing the heights
   Of glorious love
Discovering I'm seated
   With Christ
In heaven above.

Far above dark
   Schemes and snares
No more looking down
   On my self
I now see Christ
   And His wonders in me.

Surprised such love
   Made me free
Even more surprised

A Divine RE– The More Excellent Way

His love flows
Through me.

Love's expression
   Full of hope and joy.
Love expressed through
   Kindness exemplified.
Love reaching out
   To show another
The More Excellent Way.

For Love came
   Love comes again
Light of Love over darkness
   Always wins.

1

A DIVINE RE–

The landscape changed and our view as well. Randy and I stepped out into the unknown. Three times in five years we faced new territory of dirt plots overrun with weeds. In the middle between the known and unknown, a different path appeared. I process as a scribe. The Lord has woven a scarlet thread through visions, dreams, words, and the Word.

Heaven has summoned us into *A Divine Re–*

Sojourners of faith are invited to ascend the mountain of the Lord, through the valley of unfamiliar places.

The unfamiliar may be laden with shadows of loneliness, isolation, and other dark emotions.

This is where the Door of Hope beaming with Light opens to teach us the ways of the Lord.

God is Love, and it is Love beckoning us to come follow and see.

A Divine Re-

Papa, help us ... deliver us ...take us ... lift us.
Bring us out,
Bring us up,
Reform your people.

Re-order my day,
Re-order my way.

Re-make my heart,
Re-make my start.

Reveal Your plan,
Re-establish Your hand.

Recommit I do to You,
Reunited to Your truth.

Restore my destiny,
Re-lift me on Your wings.

Re-boot my capacity,
Re-launch into heavenlies.

Reignited burning bright,
Re-awakened Holy Light.

Re-calibrated move forward,
Returned to You Lord.

Re-aligned for Your Divine,
Re-purposed to shine. [1]

---

1 June 13, 2019

A promise for A Divine Re- is this word from Jeremiah 31:25:

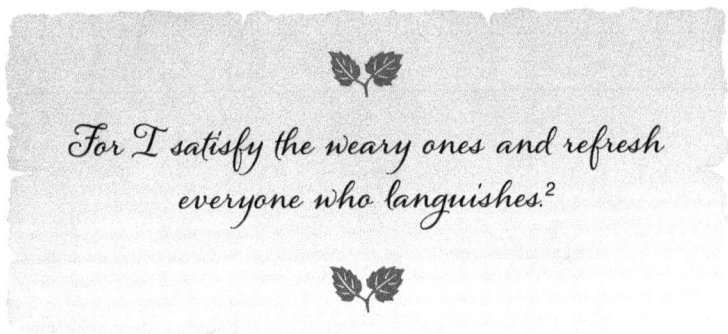

For I satisfy the weary ones and refresh everyone who languishes.[2]

These revelations are not for me alone, but I am to share. An authentic life is discovered in dying daily to self. It is also found in the sufferings of this life, which become the pathway to glorious victory.

Divine: Manifesting the essence of God's character.

The prefix RE- holds a mystery the key of revelation unlocks.

RE- to rest on, regards to, depend on, regarding…

The eyes that see heaven turn aside to His invitation.

---

2 Jeremiah 31:25 NASB

My Reflections

2

AN EPIPHANY

Even if the mountains were to crumble
 and the hills disappear,
 my heart of steadfast, faithful love
 will never leave you,
 and my covenant of peace with you will never be shaken,"
 says Yahweh,
 whose love and compassion will never give up on you.[3]

To understand the meaning of this verse, let's look at the footnote in *The Passion Translation* regarding peace:

> This is the covenant of shalom that God has made with us, his people. God's covenant promise is that his *shalom* ("peace, prosperity, success, wholeness, and well-being") will be our portion all our days on earth. (See Ephesians 2:14.)

Ephesians 2:14 (TPT) reveals Jesus is our reconciling peace:

> *Our reconciling "Peace" is Jesus! He has made Jew and non-Jew one in Christ.* ***By dying as our sacrifice,*** *he has broken down every wall of prejudice that separated us and* ***has now made us equal through our union with Christ.***

---
3 Isaiah 54:10

After meditating on this scripture and our covenant of peace, I began to have an epiphany. A manifestation of fluttering above my head—it felt like little wisps of wings or breath upon my "parietal lobe".

This part of the brain, the parietal lobe, has the following functions:

- ◊ interprets language, words
- ◊ sense of touch, pain, temperatures (sensory strip)
- ◊ interprets signals from vision, hearing, motor sensory and memory
- ◊ spatial and visual perception

An Epiphany is:

- ◊ an appearance or manifestation, especially of deity
- ◊ a sudden, intuitive perception of or insight into…
- ◊ a moment of revelation[4]

---

4 Definitions from dictionary.com

3

WINGS OF HOPE

Beloved,

The Lord will come in unusual ways to see if we will turn aside to encounter Him in His dimension. We see this in His Word.

On February 19, 2019, I had an epiphany, which has marked my journey. Yet, even more, I believe it is a mark of the emerging epoch on God's calendar for His people.

I was in my office, packing and completing things for our imminent move. All of a sudden, my eyes caught two eagles landing in the field across from my home. This was not unusual, but what transpired over the next three hours was. I grabbed my binoculars and stepped outside on my porch to view these two eagles. They were beautiful.

I went back to my office. Within moments, three more eagles came. They kept flying in until there were 12 eagles. We had never seen this many eagles together, certainly not in the field across from our home. This was a phenomenon. The presence of the Lord surrounded me. I went to my porch filled with wonder. Happy tears and giggles of sheer pleasure, as the presence of the Lord filled my heart with joy. I could feel our Father's delight, the goodness of our God. These were His gifts of tangible love and grace.

I knew this was a pivotal moment.

Wings of Hope

Letting go
   Sorting through
What I'd held close
   Tightly protected
Re-leasing to You.

   Suddenly, I see
     Two eagles
I stop
   I watch.

Then three
   And four
Now seven
   Until twelve
Upon their perch
   Watching me.

As pure snow falls
   Your voice of Love
Speaks to my weary heart
   Wrapping me in shelter.

Your presence
   Resting upon me
In me
   Filling my heart and soul.

Oh my, twelve eagles
Watching me!

Trusting, I sit
   I wait
I listen
   I hear.

Love closes a chapter
   Well done.
Now let it go
   Walk with Me
Even though
   You cannot see.

There is a path
   In letting go
Opening the way.

Another chapter
   To write
Another way to see
   With big picture eyes
From above
   Enlarging your view.

Your story of life
   Is not for you alone.
I fashion, I form
   In My hands
An eternal plan.

Will you live for Me?
   Fully yielded
Surrendering all

Letting go of what was
Turning towards
What will be?

Now I watch
Each eagle soar away
On wings a message
Begins to appear
Love turns the page.

Arise into the future
Soar with Me
On wings of hope
Through the open door.

The Lord had given me revelation about the Apostolic Glory coming. He spoke to me and told me that these 12 eagles were a divine marker alerting us we have entered this time. You can find that word on my website: intrepidheart.org.

The Lord appears in unusual ways to see if we will turn aside to encounter Him. His heavenly dimension will open to us, inviting us to *'come and see.'* His Word reveals many diverse encounters.

4

THE MORE EXCELLENT WAY

*But earnestly desire the greater gifts.
And I show you still a more excellent way.*

1 Corinthians 12:31 NASB

*But you should all constantly boil over with passion in seeking the higher gifts.
And now I will show you a superior way to live that is beyond comparison.*

1 Corinthians 12:31 TPT

The More Excellent Way is a Superior Way, beyond comparison.

The footnote in *The Passion Translation* says:
"Or a path corresponding to transcendence."

The biblical meaning of transcendence is:
Strong's Greek 5235 huperballó

Definition: to throw over or beyond, to run beyond

Usage: I surpass, excel, exceed, transcend, exceeding, pass.[5]

---

5 https://biblehub.com/greek/5235

From huper and ballo; to throw beyond the usual mark, i.e. (figuratively) to surpass (only active participle supereminent) – exceeding, excel, pass.

We can also look at this definition for transcendence:

The quality or state of being transcendent.

Transcendent means:

- Going beyond ordinary limits; surpassing; exceeding
- Superior or extreme[6]

I personally have gone through many trials, faced many tests, and I have made countless mistakes. I keep choosing to learn. I choose to learn to love. I realize learning to love is to continue to pursue the More Excellent Way. It is a search I hope to pursue all my days.

The More Excellent Way is learning the way of Love. Love is a person. One of the Lord's names is Jehovah Ahava; God is Love. Learning to love is choosing to be a *Love Slave*. It is freely yielding and surrendering. It is stretching out my arms and going where He leads me.

Yoked to Jesus
Surrendered
Yielded to Holy Spirit
Praying and doing: Lord, I give You all.

---

6 Dictionary.com

5

GAME CHANGER

In the fall of 2018, the Lord spoke this word to me. I heard it as an announcement as I watched and listened.

> It Is a Game Changer Season!

HEAR what the Father is saying to us:

> Step up to the plate and get ready to swing! Those who have aligned with Me cannot miss.
>
> You have been in My training camp. At times you have fallen—but you fell forward! You have been injured in the game of life. At times moved off the playing field and put on the bench.
>
> But I came as your Healer and bound up your wounds as you embraced the process. You have been strengthened through each exercise of faith. In your strength training, you were empowered with My supernatural might and ability. I enable you to follow the coaching and leading I provide.
>
> Get ready to swing again. IT'S A GAME CHANGER MOMENT!

HEAR what His heart is speaking to ours.

His church—His Ekklesia (which means His faithful people,) looked like the underdog. It looked like we were down and out. But the game has changed.

We have a new playbook.

It's your turn to bat, so step up! The Lord is moving you to the front and walking with you to the plate. You will recognize your perfect pitch.

I saw the enemy trying to get us to swing…demons shouting "Batter, batter, batter, swing!" Then I saw the Father put His arms around us with His hands on ours, enabling us to hit the fireball right out the park!

As we yielded to Him, we could not miss. What was supposed to strike us out became the homerun that freed us from the stadium of confinement.

The enemy tried to take us out with his fire. He tried to confine us. He attempted a strikeout. But the glory fire of God is transforming us. The fire of revival and reformation is going into the earth instead.

We are no longer benched or boxed in. Your eyes will see how to hit the mark! We soar with Holy love, right over the fence into the harvest.

HEAR the Father's invitation:

    Step-out, Step-up, Step into your game changer moment.

Every promise of God is waiting to burst forth. Hope is breaking you out. Faith is breaking you through. Love is breaking forth with the glory of God.

You are in the flame of consuming Love. You will soar as His sent one. Those who embrace the process will coach those choosing to come to Him in this move of Re- forming Love.

We will see stadiums of Lovelutionaries. We will witness massive salvations in the streets. We will release the Kingdom of Heaven. We will transform culture. We will follow the Holy One with fierce love and devotion into every sphere of society.

There will be unprecedented miracles and salvations. You have a place if you choose. You are invited:

> Rise-up off the bench of isolation.
> Step-up to the plate and join your team!
> Swing with the Lord, you cannot miss!
> Believe and move past the disappointment.

I have one compelling focus: I forget all of the past as I fasten my heart to the future instead. I run straight for the divine invitation of reaching the heavenly goal and gaining the victory-prize through the anointing of Jesus.[7]

Cheering you on!

> *Yahweh is Re-introducing the ancient way in this new day.*
> *A new playbook is Re-placing the old.*

---
7 Phil. 3:13b-14 TPT

My Reflections

6

TRANSCENDENT LOVE

The more excellent way requires trust. It is a superior pathway carved out by Love. This way transcends natural understanding and thoughts. Ephesians 3:14-21 is a holy prayer Paul prayed. For us it is a heavenly blueprint to be apprehended. *The Passion Translation*, a beautiful poetic translation of the Bible, expands upon the wisdom of God presented in these verses.

So I kneel humbly in awe before the Father of our Lord Jesus, the Messiah, the perfect Father of every father and child in heaven and on the earth. And I pray that he would unveil within you the unlimited riches of his glory and favor until supernatural strength floods your innermost being with his divine might and explosive power.

Then, by constantly using your faith, the life of Christ will be released deep inside you, and the resting place of his love will become the very source and root of your life.

Then you will be empowered to discover what every holy one experiences—the great magnitude of the astonishing love of Christ in all its dimensions. How deeply intimate and far-reaching is his love! How enduring and inclusive it is! Endless love beyond measurement that transcends our understanding—this extravagant love pours into you until you are filled to overflowing with the fullness of God!

A Divine RE- The More Excellent Way

> *Never doubt God's mighty power to work in you and accomplish all this. He will achieve infinitely more than your greatest request, your most unbelievable dream, and exceed your wildest imagination! He will outdo them all, for his miraculous power constantly energizes you.*
>
> *Now we offer up to God all the glorious praise that rises from every church in every generation through Jesus Christ—and all that will yet be manifest through time and eternity. Amen!*

Verses 18-19 highlight the wondrous experience of God's transcending love through Christ.

> *Then you will be empowered to discover what every holy one experiences—the great magnitude of the astonishing love of Christ in all its dimensions. How deeply intimate and far-reaching is his love! How enduring and inclusive it is! Endless love beyond measurement that transcends our understanding—this extravagant love pours into you until you are filled to overflowing with the fullness of God!*

To really grasp this, let us look again at the meaning of transcend:

> To surpass, excel, exceed

Transcend: the more excellent way.

Sitting with the Lord, His Spirit began to take me into the realm of supernatural wisdom and understanding. I could feel my heart expanding as my soul rejoiced in Christ. My spirit stirred to soar wherever the Lord would direct. As He had me scribe the next prose, I awakened to transcendent love. Let Him reveal Himself to you in His Logos Word in Ephesians shared previously and His Rhema—God-breathed word—shared through my encounter with this revelation.

Courtesy is nice,
But nice can be fake.
What is real
Has depths of kindness.
No mask of pretense,
Looking for something for self.
For real love
Transcends human effort.
It is Most Excellent
And never fails.
Even when the vessel fails,
The One who fills the vessel never does.
The One who is transcendent,
Far above ALL else,
Eternally good,
Full of wisdom and grace,
More than enough
To set us free.
Even when captive,
Not able to see,
Transcendent love rescues,
Reaching past to bring through.
When I cannot,
Transcendent love can.
And transcendent love
Will come through.

Discovering His more excellent way is becoming free from confining structures. We must remember that integral to this process is connecting with His body and being a part of His family.

A Divine RE- The More Excellent Way

We were not created to go it alone. For to Love, there must be a 'one another'. We need community.

I love You, Lord. Let me live in integrity wrapped in Your glorious—victorious Love.

7

SIGN OF POWER

In March 2019, I was ministering in the outskirts of Rio de Janeiro the night Carnaval started. Debbie Healy was with me. We were at a newer church. A passionate, prophetic/apostolic ministry I had not been to before. It began to rain heavily during the service. Rain was coming through the roof. The power went out for a moment during worship. It was only out briefly.

The service was powerful. God moved through prophecy, miracles, words of knowledge, signs and wonders. At the end of the service, the senior leader shared this testimony:

> When the power went out, it went out all over the region. It was still out. The only place in the community with light, with power, was the church.

This was an old building they had just begun to refurbish. They did not have a generator.

I felt it was a word for the church, the Power of God will not go out and His Light is shining bright in the darkness!

It was still pouring rain, and the streets were overflowing with rain; some flooded so much you could not drive. The power was out in the entire region except in the church.

The RE-Generation coming forth from A Divine RE- are those who walk in the power of God's Love. They will Love God with all their heart, strength, and energy to walk with Him wherever He leads. The power of God's love will never go out of His church because He is the Head of His church and He fills the Body with Himself.

He is Light, His Light is Life, and His power is in His Life.

May the Spirit of the Lord, the Spirit of Wisdom and Understanding, the Spirit of Counsel and Might, the Spirit of Knowledge and the Fear of the Lord lead you into all Truth through the blood of the Lamb of God!

8

RE-CALIBRATE

Lord,
Bring us into Your fountain of grace—Your glory flow.

Instead of our failures,

    Our misses,

        Our messes…

We come into Your rhythm,

    Your time,

        Your purpose.

Help us to RE- calibrate with your wheels of destiny—Your great grace.

Re- turn…return to the cross. Return to the contemplative life.
This age of cellular is wonderful; but it also disrupts us.
Social media becomes a boasting, busy part-time obsession.
The cellular waves disrupt peace.

To-do lists can block the tender path of intimacy. Distractions disrupt our rhythm with the One we are to behold.

Beholding Re-forms us into His image. Let us run and surrender to as *The Message* says: "the unforced rhythms of grace".

 *A Divine RE– The More Excellent Way*

"Are you tired? Worn out? Burned out on religion? Come to me. Get away with me and you'll recover your life. I'll show you how to take a real rest. Walk with me and work with me—watch how I do it. Learn the **unforced** rhythms of grace. I won't lay anything heavy or ill-fitting on you. Keep company with me and you'll learn to live freely and lightly." [8]

When we yield our hearts in steadfast pursuit to the One who is tender and strong, we come into His rhythms. His voice centers us.

Dream a little dream
Water it with hope
Don't ever stop believing
With eyes of faith, keep seeing.

---

8 Matthew 11:28-30 MSG

9

SILENCE IS STILL

Surrender your anxiety! Be silent and stop your striving and you will see that I am God. I am the God above all the nations, and I will be exalted throughout the whole earth.
— Psalm 46:10 (TPT)

Silence is our only friend at times. Silence is still, quiet, and non-intrusive. Silence would leave me alone with my thoughts. In the still, silent moments, God made Himself known to me in the depth of His way.

My appointed time in the Redondo Condo became special moments of awakening to stillness. I went deeper in silence before the Lord. I spent time worshipping, walking, praying, reading the Word. Watching the dolphins. I received from the Lord in abiding without striving. I was free from needing to make something happen.

The Power of Silence

Wisdom sits with our Father. Allowing Holy Spirit to lead in silence—when to speak—when to be silent—listening—leaning—praying—bending in flexibility.

Not needing to be the one seen, but living for "The ONE" to be seen, felt, heard, and known.

Endless chatter loses the TRUTH heart of the matter. It requires humility, bowing, and bending the knee. Leaning the heart into His heart. This is where the Truth, the Way, and the Life are made visible. Christ longs to lead us in every aspect of life.

His Love Light shining upon us,
> Illuminating what is of Him to be kept and hidden.
> Discerning what is to be shared.
> Revealing what is not of Him and to be flushed away.
> It is in silence that which is His 'Now' revelation, once hidden and 'Now' *Revealed*.
> In stillness of Love's presence, what needs time to develop appears.

*The Lord God has given Me the tongue
of disciples,
So that I may know how to sustain the
weary one with a word.
He awakens Me morning by morning,
He awakens My ear to listen as a disciple.
The Lord God has opened My ear,
And I was not disobedient,
Nor did I turn back.*[9]

---

9 Isaiah 50:4-5 NASB

Christ is Wisdom, Wisdom sits with Our Father, and we are seated with Christ, Wisdom.

My revelation-truth is a gift to you,
so remain faithful to my instruction.

Stick with wisdom and she will stick to you,
protecting you throughout your days.
She will rescue all those who passionately listen to her voice.
Wisdom is the most valuable commodity—so buy it!
Revelation knowledge is what you need—so invest in it!
Wisdom will exalt you when you exalt her truth.
She will lead you to honor and favor
when you live your life by her insights.
You will be adorned with beauty and grace,
and wisdom's glory will wrap itself around you,
making you victorious in the race.

But the lovers of God walk on the highway of light,
and their way shines brighter and brighter
until they bring forth the perfect day.[10]

---

10 Proverbs 4:2, 6-9 and 18 TPT

My Reflections

10

TO SIT AND BE

To sit and be
What does this mean?
It's not inactivity
But life flowing
From rest and trust.
Seated above
Right next to love
A holy flowetic
From River to vine
Divine union
Life from communion.

Connect
At rest
Weaknesses covered
Holy blood life
Healing leaves
Trees of standing right
Planted
Flourishing
Not moved by storms
Authority established
Legislate Truth.

Undivided no more
Fully united
Whole and free
Free to be
Happy, joyful holiness
Bright Light
Shining bright.

Though darkness assails
Christ's Holy Love Light
Chases darkness into day
The dawn of new life
Awakening dreamers
To see
To believe
To receive
To sit and to be.

11

HOOPS AND SYSTEMS

The Lord spoke, "No more hoops. You are not to jump through anyone's hoops anymore". I was preparing to host an event with a well-known speaker and leader. I respect and esteem this person. The Lord was preparing me for a test.

Hoops are high expectations. Parts of the church are more of an entertainment arena than a healing equipping center. Hoops and systems measure and compare. There are many dead dreams and wounded hearts on ash heaps of measuring and comparing.

A Divine Re- is an invitation from our Father to Re-evaluate if we are on His path.

'Religious duty' is one of the hoops God is exposing. Religious duty produces performance-based Christianity. When measured by man's standards, we might assess ourselves as failures. The fruit of this can be insecurity. Comparison is done at many meetings. For example: look at the numbers, the money, even the crowd response.

> We are not to find our assessment of who we are from people. We are becoming who HE SAYS WE ARE.
> I hear The Lord say: The Promised Land is Heaven's Vision for our life.

It is our God-given desire to be free to breathe. To know what words, appointments, assignments, and alignments are divinely His.

His truth implanted in our souls reveals our true calling.
>Disciples—Sons and Daughters—Lovers of God.

I scribed in June 2019:

> I'm pondering the many hoops, systems: political and religious, which plague the Lord's beautiful body. These systems cause pain, anger, and frustration to those who will be His Bride. I'm pondering this season, this hour—the Lord's history and words.

How many misfits and outcasts…
I hear the One I love say:

> Help My sons and daughters be set free from the noose of performance and religion.

I entered a season of deep groaning of Holy Spirit and intense intercession. Through prophetic insight and words spoken over my role in this birthing of God's heart intentions, I pressed through some intense moments. The Word of God, written and spoken, are hope lifelines.

> *You're my place of quiet retreat,*
> *and your wrap-around presence*
> *becomes my shield as I wrap myself in your word!*
> *Lord, strengthen my inner being*
> *by the promises of your word*
> *so that I may live faithful and unashamed for you.*
> *Lift me up and I will be safe.*

Empower me to live every moment in the light of your ways. [11]

Embrace the transforming power of Holy Spirit as teacher, friend, and guide. He is with us in every season.

Jesus is taking us into His thoughts and ways. He is delivering us from self-preservation and what man calls security. He is releasing us into radical obedience motivated by love. His love for us infuses our love for Him.

This is the *no fear of man* and *no fear of failure* realm of the Kingdom. Living in and from the heart of our Father's love.

Christianity is not a competition; it is collaboration.

> It was never meant to be a talent show; it is to be a heavenly orchestration of Love flowing to us from Christ Jesus. Union with Christ Jesus releases His Life to flow through us.

---

11 Psalm 119:114, 116-117 TPT

My Reflections

12

PARIAH

People everywhere feel like a pariah. When I felt this in the atmosphere, I looked up the word.

Pariah means:
> any person or animal that is generally despised or avoided an outcast
>> a member of a low caste in Southern India and Burma[12]

Oh, my goodness, what have we done? It's as if we have perpetuated the 'avoid the leper and keep them outside the camp' mindset.

People are not pariahs. Each person is a gift regardless of whether they are up to others' standards.

The way Jesus walked right up to the leper, the outcast, the rejected, and those society deemed undesirable reveals the heart of our Father. We need His heart.

We need to discern each other rightly, through the redemptive eyes of Love. Whether someone is hidden or known is not the measure of value in the Lord's eyes.

From 'other' to 'one another'

---

12 Dictionary.com

A Divine RE– The More Excellent Way

My Reflections

13

THE SIN-BEARER

I was pondering a spiritual dilemma—the way many Christians look at sinners and deem them lepers, untouchable, or unclean.

Yet, Jesus died to cleanse all: the lepers, the unclean, and sinners.

We are to "Be" Him on the earth.

I began to sing in the spirit:

You welcomed Your Bride
Through Your split open side.
Pierced through,
Your blood made the way
With You we abide.

I heard Jesus speak to me as I sat to read His Word, "Read my sacrificial account of atonement in John 18 and 19."

When I read John 19:33-34, I was undone. Here was His Word expressing the very thing He was speaking to me and singing through me.

> *But when they came to Jesus, they realized that he had already died, so they decided not to break his legs.*
>
> *But one of the soldiers took a spear and pierced Jesus' side, and blood and water gushed out.* [13]

---

13 John 19:33-34 TPT

The Footnote for verse 34: This becomes a picture of the cleansing by blood and the water of the Holy Spirit. However, water and blood both come forth when a baby is born. Christ gave birth on the cross to "sons." He is the everlasting Father (Isa. 9:6), and you must have children to be a Father. We are all born again by the wounded side of Jesus Christ. He not only died for his bride, but he also gave birth to her at the cross.

Isaiah 51 tells us to "look at the Rock from which you were hewn." Song of Solomon chapter 2 speaks about being hidden in the cleft of the Rock. We are hidden in the Rock Christ Jesus. Jesus, the Rock, was split open to bring us into a born-again relationship with Our Father.

How can we look at the 'other' and not see the 'one another' for which He died? We have de-humanized people by putting labels of sin on their identity. This is the work of the devil. It is time we remember to be like Jesus, releasing peace and forgiveness and encouraging them to find their identity in Him.

> *So when it was evening on that day, the first day of the week, and when the doors were shut where the disciples were, for fear of the Jews, Jesus came and stood in their midst and said to them, "Peace be with you."*
>
> *And when He had said this, He showed them both His hands and His side. The disciples then they saw the Lord.*
>
> *So Jesus said to them again, "Peace be with you; as the Father has sent Me, I also send you."*
>
> *And when He had said this, He breathed on them and said to them, "Receive the Holy Spirit.*

> *"If you forgive the sins of any, their sins have been forgiven them; if you retain the sins of any, they have been retained."* [14]

It is time to have Re-newed vision, to see with Love's eyes. To Remember why He was pierced and split-open.

The Sin-Bearer Servant

> Yet he was the one who carried our sicknesses
> and endured the torment of our sufferings.
> We viewed him as one who was being punished
> for something he himself had done,
> as one who was struck down by God and brought
> low. But it was because of our rebellious deeds that
> he was pierced
> and because of our sins that he was crushed.
>
> He endured the punishment that made us
> completely whole,
> and in his wounding, we found our healing.
> Like wayward sheep, we have all wandered astray.
> Each of us has turned from God's paths and chosen our
> own way;
> even so, Yahweh laid the guilt of our every sin upon him. [15]

It is possible to love the sinner and hate the sin.
Jesus never celebrated sin. He confronted sin with truth. Truth –
He is Truth. Truth sets us free. Truth breaks chains.
Jesus so full of love, with His eyes on our Father, set captives free.
Never compromised.

---

14 John 20:19-23
15 Isaiah 53:4-6

Always loving.
Always steady.
Always faithful to the Word of God, as He is the Word of God. [16]

"May we be enabled to say "no" to sin and "Yes" to the sinner. May we withstand our foes, and yet hold out to the Word of the gospel which woos and wins the souls of men."

Dietrich Bonhoeffer

Jesus the Light shined light into darkness.
The Greater Light caused shadows to flee.
Come into the Light.
Receive the Light of Truth.
   Then be the light.

Let us light up the darkness as our lights become one in Him.

Arise, shine! For your light has come. And the glory of the LORD shines upon you[17]

---

16 Yom Kippur September 28, 2020
17 (See Isaiah 60:1)

14

IDENTITY
GENUINE – REAL

Identity is not in what we do, but who we are.

Who am I in the dream of I Am?

Discovering this is liberating and empowering. It happens when we rest and trust. Rest and trust unlock the ability to see the truth about being a son or daughter.

We are not puppets. Yet, the one who steals the dreams of I Am attempts to keep us on his puppet master strings. His strings are lies capturing us in dark traps and snares. The puppet master manipulates us to be copycat performers.

It's the trap of the next 'who's who', of 'watcha ma call it' grandiose scheme.

It's the age-old lies of:
> If only you did this or that…if only you were this way-always falling short.

It's a merry-go-round spinning under the control of fear. It is a 'never-good-enough' mindset which produces performance-based behaviors such as wanting to fit in and please others. This spinning

 *A Divine RE- The More Excellent Way*

round and round is greased with human reasoning and self-made agendas. It is a company of pretenders pretending and chanting:

"I am ok", "You are not, so get out of the way, or I will roll over you to get my way into the place and position I desire."

WAIT—STOP—

TRUTH TIME-OUT

To be free of this we need to be RE-aligned with Truth.

There is more than enough in this pie of life.

I need you—they, the 'one anothers' we are called to love, need you too.

Together we can bring healing and liberty.

As we make way and make room for each other, we multiply in grace and love.

Oh, for the freedom to have real, genuine, organic relationship, founded on the grace and love of God.

15

THE MEASURE OF GRACE

Christ is our measure. Whether we measure up or fall short in another's eyes is not how we are to find self-worth. Jesus is the plumb line.

"Mary Poppins" is a whimsical story, inspiring hope. As much as I love the movie, the scene where Mary Poppins brings out her measuring tape disturbs me. She proceeds to measure the children and describe the places they do not measure up. When she holds the measuring tape up to herself she proclaims the words, "Mary Poppins, practically perfect in every way."

For the sake of the fictional story, this is 'all good.' But in real life, this is often what we do to each other: We carry a measuring tape in our baggage. We measure others with high standards through critical lenses based on our beliefs and biases. To top it off, we compare others with our measuring tools. This breeds contempt and jealousy. Our standards can be impossible to attain. We might look at ourselves and estimate we are without fault or blemish. The opposite could be true in some of our lives. We measure ourselves with extreme criticism and self-loathing as we compare ourselves to

those around us. We esteem them all together perfect and ourselves wretched failures.

We forget our measuring tape originates from our baggage.

We often fictionalize the mess of our lives with the statement 'It's all good,' when everything is not. It is at those times we need the measure of grace. God, in His goodness, will work all things out for good. But this does not mean everything is 'all good.'

> *And we know that God causes all things to work together for good to those who love God, to those who are called according to His purpose. For those whom He foreknew, He also predestined to become conformed to the image of His Son, so that He would be the firstborn among many brethren.*[18]

We need the measure of grace.

When we measure others through critical lenses, we miss the beauty of process. A tree starts as a seed, and it needs to be planted in prepared soil. It then begins the process of rooting, grounding, and growing. As it grows, it requires nurturing, water, sunshine, and time. A vital aspect of the process is weeding, feeding ,and pruning.

When we are rooted and grounded in God's love, we will grow in true discernment towards others.

The church needs the plumb line of Jesus. With His 'measure of grace' in whatever sphere of influence you are called to. We tend to measure each other by what and how we do life, comparing how we do ministry, how much (money), how big (the building is), etc. We are not called to a cookie cutter kind of ministry. God has given each of us the grace to do what He made us to do.

---

18 Romans 8:28-29

Knowing our sphere of influence helps us to walk in the measure He has given us.

> *God has given me grace to speak a warning about pride. I would ask each of you to be emptied of self-promotion and not create a false image of your importance. Instead, honestly assess your worth by using your God-given faith as the standard of measurement, and then you will see your true value with an appropriate self-esteem.*[19]

Putting away the ruler of comparison sets us free to be who we are called to be and to only do what the Father shows us.

We need to re-establish the standard of the Golden Rule. A measuring stick is called a ruler. Are we "ruled" by others' measurements of us, or our measurements of them? What if we allow the Golden Rule founded on Matthew 7:1-5, and 12 to be the measure of grace released in our lives and others?

> *When we judge or measure after our own ideals, we open the door for offense. Offense blocks grace. Offense is rooted in pride. God resists the proud, yet He graces the humble. Humility is the path to live in our individual and corporate measure of grace...We have all the grace we need to be in our lane.*[20]

In an age where performance and gifting has been elevated above humility and a servant's heart, let us re-evaluate our measures. For ourselves individually, we can choose to come to the fullness of the measure of Christ. Christ is our measure, not man's systems. In regard to others, let us see them through the lenses of His measure of grace.

---

19 Romans 12:3 TPT
20 Matthew 7:1-5, 12 TPT

>
>
> *But to each one of us grace was given according to the measure of Christ's gift.*[21]
>
>

Perhaps when we recognize the measure of Christ's gift in each other, we can decree we are *'being made perfect in Christ and His ways!'*

---

21 Ephesians 4:7

16

PERFECT

I hear the Lord saying,

> I knew you wouldn't do it perfectly.
> Perfect obedience comes only from Me.
> Ask Me for help
> Then let My perfect record accomplish what
> needs to happen.
> For I am the God who heals thee
> Who comforts thee
> Who sets you free.
> My perfect record sets yours straight.
> Receive the promise,
> Say yes and amen!

How I long for my life to bring you glory
as I follow each and every one of your holy precepts. [22]

---

[22] Psalm 119:5 TPT

My Reflections

17

IMAGINE BRANDING JESUS

I heard this funny phrase—
>   Imagine branding Jesus… [23]

Here is the Savior of the World: He moves in power, heals the sick, raises the dead, and encourages the people.

>   Imagine branding Jesus
>   He's the one who will save the day!
>   He heals
>   He delivers
>   He comes to make a way
>
>   But wait
>   He is not doing it our way
>   The religious cry out
>   The political fear
>
>   He doesn't fit the mold
>   To pressure He won't bow His knee
>   He overturns our moneymaking tables
>   He sets the captives free
>   The ones we deem less than desirable
>   Where we turn our heads and walk away-

---
23 February 11, 2020

 *A Divine RE– The More Excellent Way*

> He stops
> He stoops
> He looks and sees
> Healing every need.

The ones branding would find themselves at a loss for who He hangs out with, how he speaks to the religious, how He writes secrets in the sand revealing the dark heart motives of the self-righteous. They may be perplexed when He gets in boats and leaves the crowds. The branding coach might find himself frustrated with Jesus' confidence and unwavering faith in a Father no one has seen, except the One they are trying to promote and give an acceptable image.

Who is this Jesus?

In a world where we image and brand a multitude of products and people, how would you brand Jesus? Examining this question will expose some of the ways we are promoting the sale of the gospel and its message today. More so, as it relates to us, it is very easy for this exercise of branding to become a form of self-promotion. We need the sifter of truth poured out with grace.

> *It is the greatest joy of my life to hear that my children are consistently living their lives in the ways of truth![24]*
> *Love does not brag about one's achievements nor inflate its own importance.[25]*

John 14:6 states:
> *Jesus explained, "I am the Way, I am the Truth, and I am the Life. No one comes next to the Father except through union with me. To know me is to know my Father too. [26]*

---

24 3 John 4 TPT
25 1 Corinthians 13:4b TPT
26 TPT

His way for us as individuals is best. When we behold Him in His presence, we will find His way, through His truth, and full of His life. This will cause us to become like Him!

> *Now, the "Lord" I'm referring to is the Holy Spirit, and wherever he is Lord, there is freedom. We can all draw close to him with the veil removed from our faces. And with no veil we all become like mirrors who brightly reflect the glory of the Lord Jesus. We are being transfigured into his very image as we move from one brighter level of glory to another. And this glorious transfiguration comes from the Lord, who is the Spirit.* [27]

Jesus is not a brand. He is the Way. He is the Son of Our Father, the One who redeems us. He chose to empty Himself of His deity and become a man to reveal the love of the Father. Branding and promotion birth a class of ministers who separate themselves from the people. Does love reject the one who comes up to the sacred row of speakers? Does the Jesus in us reach out to love and embrace? To pray until those waiting for prayer have been prayed for?

"What would Jesus do?" was a popular phrase that is still sometimes used. Find the answer to this and discover Jesus as the Truth. From His life and words, we can find the blueprint for what He would do in our world today. Jesus spoke words, and He is the Word.

> *Open your heart and consider my words. Watch out that you do not mistake your opinions for revelation-light! If your spirit burns with light, fully illuminated with no trace of darkness, you will be a shining lamp, reflecting rays of truth by the way you live."* [28]

---

[27] 2 Corinthians 3:17-18 TPT
[28] Luke 11:35-38 TPT

Branding is done to mark a belonging. It puts limitations on a person or product. We are imprinted with the fingerprint of God. The Creator's signature is upon us. The enemy tries to re-brand us and imprint his nature upon us. He limits us as he puts shackles around our souls.

Jesus is also the Life. His Life flows in us, through us, and marks us. We are marked as bondservants who RE-present the very essence of who He is.

Let us be those who leave footprints, imprints, and images of Jesus for others to see. If we would resist the copycat brand and become the authentic follower of Jesus, He will be made famous in our day!

Authenticity is not the next fad.
It is a life laid down to love and serve.
Get real
and
Be real!

18

JESUS' BLOOD SPEAKS

The voice of the blood
Upon the cross of shame
Shame—humiliation
A cursed tree
The blood-stained cross
A man hung
Condemned for being
Too good
   Too right

He wouldn't fight
Nor raise a voice of condemnation
Nor defend Himself

His blood
His voice
Speaking a better word!

The Word:
Cleansing
Freedom
Healing
Deliverance
Salvation
Acceptance
Beloved

The blood speaks
As one was pierced
Upon the cross

The voice of the Word crying out
Forgiven
Mine
Redeemed
Purchased
Free

Father's love
Christ's blood
Mercy, mercy

Today paradise lost
Is paradise found.

Power in the Blood of Jesus
No curse can alight because of the blood of Jesus.
No curse of sickness, debt, fear, or lack… NO Curse!
Restored, healed, delivered and empowered through the blood of Jesus.
Receive His Oil of Glory—His Life—His Empowering Grace!

19

YOU'RE SOMETHING! WHO ARE YOU?

I had a dream on March 27, 2020. A significant part of the dream is not just for me, but for His people.

I was being introduced to a credible, well-known prophet. He looked up at me and said:

"You're something! Who are you?"

He then began to speak to me. At the end of what he said, he pushed me out the door and I awoke.

When I sat with the Lord regarding this dream, He reminded me that this prophet had given me a word in August 2003. The word started with the prophet saying:

"You're something! What's your name?"

The only difference between the two experiences was instead of 'who are you?' it was, 'what's your name?' Both identify who the Lord says we are and what we are called to do. The Lord then spoke to me that this word was for now. The word prophesied who I am and explained why I'm the quirky way God made me. There were many promises in the word.

A Divine RE- The More Excellent Way

The Lord instructed me to tell His people, "You're something! Who are you?" Who does the Lord say we are? He is calling us by name. He looks at you and sees someone of great value and worth. As you realize He is calling you into your identity as a son or daughter, He is looking at His marvelous image in you. You're something—you bear the image of wonder. Our Father created us and put His very nature into us.

We can be assured every promise He has given us is yes and amen.

You're Something! And NOW He is releasing us to go and tell people **Who He Says They Are.**

20

WHO ARE YOU?

In this Divine RE- the Lord is calling His people out of conformity, performance, perfectionism, elitism, and other debilitating strongholds of manmade systems. He is asking, "Do you really want to be part of the "who's who" of the church culture fame game?"

We may wrestle with being known. We may wrestle with not-being known. Let Christ win the wrestle. We seek Him and His Kingdom. We seek to make Him known. Knowing Him reveals who we are.

If He lifts us to a place of prominence, let our hearts remain in His posture of humility. Let love rule and guide our ways. Let us remember the 'one anothers.'

> So I'm asking you, my friends, that you be joined together in perfect unity—with one heart, one passion, and united in one love. Walk together with one harmonious purpose and you will fill my heart with unbounded joy.
>
> Be free from pride-filled opinions, for they will only harm your cherished unity. Don't allow self-promotion to hide in your hearts, but in authentic humility put others first and view others as more important than yourselves. Abandon every display of selfishness. Possess a greater concern for what matters to others instead of your own interests.[29]

---

[29] Philippians 2:2-4 TPT

His call: "Be at peace and be who I say you are."

No need to fit in.

You are called to fit with God, to fit with His heart and plan.

You hold the keys to unlock the harvest and open the glory gates. It is God's glory fire that routs out the enemy. Apostolic glory of laid-down lovers who know their instructions as a sent one come from the original blueprint written in their book of life.

"As long as the Lord is glorified – the servant is satisfied."

Violet Kitely

This is a powerful statement. It was Violet Kitely's motto for 70 years of ministry.

Today, many in ministry feel promotion is equivalent to being known. They desire a glorified position. In discerning this situation, reflect over the following questions: Does the minister lead people to encounter Jesus and remember Him? Or are people left with a human idol?

Who you are is the signature of God, our Father.
    His fingerprint.
        His one-of-a-kind piece of art.

Branding like the world…NO!
Signature, Fingerprint of our Father…YES!

> *Be free from pride-filled opinions, for they will only harm your cherished unity. Don't allow self-promotion to hide in your hearts, but in authentic humility put others first and view others as more important than yourselves. Abandon every display of selfishness. Possess a greater concern for what matters to others instead of your own interests. And consider the example that Jesus, the Anointed One, has set before us. Let his mindset become your motivation.* [30]

---

[30] Philippians 2:3-5 TPT

The Lord is my rock and my salvation. In Him I trust.

Whom shall I fear?
    NO ONE—no not one.

My trust is in the Lord, the creator—maker of heaven and earth.

21

SEE WHAT IS HIDDEN

The Lord is inviting us to see what has been hidden. He is releasing us from old cycles to bring us into His cycles and revolutions.

> *It is He who reveals the profound and hidden things; He knows what is in the darkness, And the light dwells with Him.*[31]

God, El-Shaddai, is doing for us what we cannot.

Breaking us free from the hamster wheel, the rat race of running in circles. Free from the exhausting, never-ending cycle of getting nowhere.

A cycle in this revelation represents appointed times.

Revolution in this revelation is the turning of a wheel, coming round, turning, due time. It also is the "Upheaval."

Both of these refer to God's appointed times and His turning points to bring about His purpose.

Now is the time we find His pathway from heaven into earth.

Jesus taught us to pray,

---

31 Daniel 2:22 NASB

A Divine RE– The More Excellent Way

> Your Kingdom come, Your will be done, On earth as it is in heaven. [32]

Here we discover His purpose and learn how to partner with His vision.

Omni-Vision: God's vision.

> His will
>> His way
>>> His plan

> His thoughts
>> His Word
>>> His Spirit

He is releasing His mighty hand to deliver His people from the enemy's cycles.

He is RE-aligning and RE-calibrating us with heaven's cycles.

Those who embrace His Divine RE are being fine-tuned to His timing and frequency.

He is resurrecting us.
I hear Him saying:

> "Talitha Kum" [33]

Eyes fixed
Vision focused
Holding steady
Standing steadfast.

---

32 Matthew 6:10 NASB
33 From Mark 5:41 NASB; Little girl, I say to you get up!

God's ways lead me to His heart, His purpose.
Omni-vision encompasses me, empowering me to see the way, the path of His plan. [34]

> *Now it came about when Joshua was by Jericho, that he lifted up his eyes and looked, and behold, a man was standing opposite him with his sword drawn in his hand, and Joshua went to him and said to him, "Are you for us or for our adversaries?" He said, "No; rather I indeed come now as captain of the host of the Lord." And Joshua fell on his face to the earth, and bowed down, and said to him, "What has my lord to say to his servant?" The captain of the Lord's host said to Joshua, "Remove your sandals from your feet, for the place where you are standing is holy." And Joshua did so.* [35]

We need God's vision, God's way. He will send help whether through His word, His friends, or perhaps even His host. His angels are sent to minister to the heirs of salvation.[36]

What is being determined as we crossover from one age to the next is, are we on the Lord's side? If so, we must realize we are on holy ground and bow before our King.

He took us out to remove the Baals, the bitterness, the false responsibility of the past age.
It's a new epoch—a major transformation is manifesting.
No one can stop the hand of God.
God is faithful.

---

34 February 23, 2020
35 Joshua 5:13-15 NASB
36 Reference Hebrews 1, especially verse 14

Yahweh—the "Vav" of heaven, is grounding us in heavenly places with heaven's perspective.[37]

"Why" is not a question I seek, or even ask. Yet 'why' is the question I have asked in this upheaval.

"Why" can be the 'Y' at the crossroads. Instead of looking at 'why' as a hopeless question, see the 'Y' in the road with Omni-vision to know which way the Lord is leading. The crossing over and into must have His direction.

Stay steady in the upheaval.

> *The steadfast of mind you will keep in perfect peace, because he trusts in you.*[38]

> *Create in me a clean heart, O God, and renew a steadfast spirit within me.*[39]

The upheaval exposes areas in our hearts. Places of fear, anger, bitterness, disappointment and other emotions, thoughts and strongholds. These places are what the Healer is coming to cleanse, heal, set-free, and transform us from and into. From darkness into light. From self-reliance into holy dependence upon His breath, His Spirit. Only Holy Spirit brings true transformation.

Transformation means:

> In theology, a change of heart in man, by which his disposition

---

37 Vav is the 6th letter of the Hebrew Aleph-Bet. It implies the connection between spiritual and earthly matters. It is the connecting force of God, the divine "hook" that binds together heaven and earth. https://www.hebrew-4christians.com/Grammar/Unit_One/Aleph-Bet/Vav/vav.html
38 Isaiah 26:3 NASB
39 Psalm 51:10 NASB

and temper are conformed to the Divine image; a change from enmity to holiness and love.[40]

Beloved friends, what should be our proper response to God's marvelous mercies? To surrender yourselves to God to be his sacred, living sacrifices. And live in holiness, experiencing all that delights his heart. For this becomes your genuine expression of worship.

Stop imitating the ideals and opinions of the culture around you, but be inwardly transformed by the Holy Spirit through a total reformation of how you think. This will empower you to discern God's will as you live a beautiful life, satisfying and perfect in his eyes. [41]

To live in the full potential of God's destiny is to get in step with Him,
    His purpose,
        His plan.

We cannot allow the pain of disappointment to rule our life.

Hope must float—faith must arise

Love will overcome!

---

40 Webster's 1828 Dictionary
41 Romans 12:1-2 TPT

My Reflections

22

UPHEAVALS … STAY STEADY

A Word of Hope and Stability

"Open the gates, that the righteous nation may enter,
The one that remains faithful.
"The steadfast of mind You will keep in perfect peace,
Because he trusts in You.
"Trust in the Lord forever,
For in God the Lord, we have an everlasting Rock.[42]

In October 2019, the Lord spoke to me in my quiet time, "Randy is getting a promotion, and it's an upheaval." The next day the company he works for announced the entire program he works on was re-locating to Utah. Yes, another "RE" in our lives.

Honestly, we felt everything in our lives shaking. We sought the Lord for His heart and plan.

On February 9, 2020, the Lord spoke to me during worship at church, "*Stay Steady*." A few moments later He said, "*Stay Steady, the next upheaval is coming.*" We have all felt the upheaval of CO-VID-19 which is what the Lord was referring too.

---

42 Isaiah 26:2-4 NASB

We also found out in February Randy's employment relied on him taking a re-location position.

To stay steady in upheaval, we need understanding.

To Stay refers to holding out, enduring, to pause, wait, stand firm.

Steady is to be firmly placed or fixed; stable in position or equilibrium;

Free from agitation; calm, firm; unfaltering.

Upheaval:

1: the action or an instance of *upheaving* especially of part of the earth's crust

2: extreme agitation or disorder: radical change[43]

An upheaval brings to the surface what is hidden. It exposes what has been under the surface. We also see in the definition that it is radical change with the aspects of extreme agitation and disorder. We are seeing this on every mountain of society.

As I sat with the Lord over these words, "*Stay Steady*", I pondered, *how do we do this?* It's good to ask questions. He kept pointing me back to what He had been speaking to me the past few months and even within the last year.

He gave me a word regarding the epoch we have entered which some call an 'era'. The word is Omni-Vision. The word Omni points to the **All** Sufficient God. He is saying we need to have God's vision. Vision to see with the Father's heart.

God's ways, not mine.

---

43 Definitions from Dictionary.com

God's thoughts and not mine…or others…so many opinions cloud our vision.

> *Let the wicked forsake his way*
> *And the unrighteous man his thoughts;*
> *And let him return to the Lord,*
> *And He will have compassion on him,*
> *And to our God,*
> *For He will abundantly pardon.*
> *"For My thoughts are not your thoughts,*
> *Nor are your ways My ways," declares the Lord.*
> *"For as the heavens are higher than the earth,*
> *So are My ways higher than your ways*
> *And My thoughts than your thoughts.*[44]

We must know Him. To know Him will give us the ability to know His heart. When we know Him this way, we will have vision to follow Him wherever and however He leads us. This gives us the ability to "*Stay Steady*" even in the midst of upheavals.

If we choose wisdom, we will remember it is the Mountain of the Lord we are called to. On this mountain we get the Lord's perspective, His view, His vision.

> *Now it will come about that*
> *In the last days*
> *The mountain of the house of the Lord*
> *Will be established as the chief of the mountains,*
> *And will be raised above the hills;*
> *And all the nations will stream to it.*
> *And many peoples will come and say,*
> *"Come, let us go up to the mountain of the Lord,*

---

44 Isaiah 55:7-9 NASB

 *A Divine RE– The More Excellent Way*

> *To the house of the God of Jacob;*
> *That He may teach us concerning His ways*
> *And that we may walk in His paths."*
> *For the law will go forth from Zion*
> *And the word of the Lord from Jerusalem.*[45]

Seated with Christ, we abide in the dwelling of God. Our position with Him gives us access to everything we need.

The Lord invited us in 2019 to enter "A Divine Re." In 2020, the way we knew to do life changed.

On March 10, 2020

I saw a huge rainbow in the sky. The Lord spoke to me His promises are 'yes' and 'amen'. This reminder establishes the ability to "Stay Steady."

We had double upheaval, which turned into a season of twists and turns we did not see coming. You may ask why the move was such an upheaval. To give context to our journey, I had waited 29 years for the fulfillment of a promise Randy made to me when he proposed to me. I met Randy during a time I had moved to Utah to get on my feet. (My mom and step-dad lived there). I had no plans of staying in Utah. When he proposed, I wanted to say yes but there were many factors I found not favorable. The biggest block was I never wanted to live in Utah. I also did not want to live somewhere with harsh winters. Randy assured me we would not live in Utah forever. In our 29th year of marriage, he was able to fulfill his proposal promise. And the Lord made it very special. My favorite place is the beach. We lived a little over an hour from the

---

45 Isaiah 2:2

beach. For five of the months in California ,Randy's work paid for a condo right on the beach in Redondo. It was a dream of mine to live near the beach and a bigger dream to live on the beach. Promises and dreams collided and the overflow of this fulfillment was happiness beyond anything I'd ever known.

The rug holding the dream in place was ripped out from under me. Everything shook. In the time before the upheaval the Lord's appointed detox had begun in my life.

With the words "*Stay Steady*" we rest in the Lord, trusting His wisdom and understanding to direct us. There are moments we have had to war with prophetic promises to steady our hearts. Other moments we have had to strive to stay in rest. The process deepens our trust in God and devotion to each other. We are staying steady with Jesus, the Anchor of our Hope.

This hope we have as an anchor of the soul, a hope both sure and steadfast and one which enters within the veil...[46]

---

46 Hebrews 6:19 NASB

A Divine RE- The More Excellent Way

My Reflections

23

A RE-SEASON

A season of Repenting and RE-turning

And now, brethren, I know that you acted in ignorance [not aware of what you were doing], as did your rulers also.

Thus has God fulfilled what He foretold by the mouth of all the prophets, that His Christ (the Messiah) should undergo ill treatment and be afflicted and suffer.

So repent (change your mind and purpose); turn around and return [to God], that your sins may be erased (blotted out, wiped clean), that times of refreshing (of recovering from the effects of heat, of reviving with fresh air) may come from the presence of the Lord;

And that He may send [to you] the Christ (the Messiah), Who before was designated and appointed for you—even Jesus,

Whom heaven must receive [and retain] until the time for the complete restoration of all that God spoke by the mouth of all His holy prophets for ages past [from the most ancient time in the memory of man].[47]

---

47 Acts 3:17-21 AMPC

Many were lulled to sleep. Many have been inoculated with doctrines of demons.

Arise, Shine –

> For your light of truth has come.

Repent and Re-turn,

there is a Door of Hope leading to salvation.

24

OMNI VISION

From Bitterness to Delight

A word from the Lord emerging on 2/22/2020 and continuing…

> *So they both went until they came to Bethlehem. And when they had come to Bethlehem, all the city was stirred because of them, and the women said, "Is this Naomi?" She said to them, "Do not call me Naomi; call me Mara, for the Almighty has dealt very bitterly with me. I went out full, but the Lord has brought me back empty. Why do you call me Naomi, since the Lord has witnessed against me and the Almighty has afflicted me?"*[48]

We are coming out of a bitter era into a sweet era. The restoration of promises found in the Name of Yahweh. Written into our DNA is the promise of hope and destiny the Father has for us. Many of us endured the last decade of disappointment and delays. We may not recognize it, yet we are returning to the land of promise. Entering the land of promise usually means we have battles to overcome. This is how we inherit the promise.

---

48 Ruth 1:19-21 NASB

The battle that began in 2020 is the epic battle, whose report will we believe…?

Yes, there is warfare. Yes, there is great darkness. And YES, God is for His people. He always prepares a path for us to discover Him in every season.

Naomi means my delight or my pleasantness.

Mara means bitterness and was a name Naomi called herself due to her calamities.[49]

Naomi did not have God's vision. The lenses of her heart were clouded by her dismal circumstances and losses.

I understand this. I should have had more joy crossing over into the unknown. I have history with God. But emotions have their own path carved out at times. Grace for how we feel in transition is a must.

We were getting established when "upheaval" came. We had new waters to navigate. The battle to remain in peace and continue to grow in sweetness became intense.

We needed to change our perspective. Often people quote the phrase "new level, new devil". I prefer the word of God to this phrase of man. The scripture reveals "new level" means the supply of new heavenly help. Moses met God at the burning bush and was supernaturally empowered with help from "I AM". Later, an angel of the Lord went before Him and the people of God. The Angel of the Lord met Joshua before crossing the river Jordan. There are many references in the Word of God of His provision and help. At Jesus' baptism He is anointed with Holy Spirit and driven into the

---

49 Strong's Greek Concordance

wilderness. At the end of testing and battle with the devil, ministering angels refreshed Jesus before He began His earthly ministry.

Many of us did not recognize the season, even the era we were in.

It is a season where He is giving us *Omni-Vision*.

Omni- Points to God, He is All encompassing.

Vision definition: In Scripture, a revelation from God; an appearance or exhibition of something supernaturally presented to the minds of the prophets, by which they were informed of future events. Such were the visions of Isaiah, of Amos, of Ezekiel, etc.[50]

Omni-vision points towards Omnipresence:

> Presence in every place at the same time; unbounded or universal presence; ubiquity. *omnipresence* is an attribute peculiar to God.[51]

Lord, help us to enter into Your courts with thanksgiving and Your presence with praise. It is in Your presence that we will see and discern with Omni-Vision the era we have entered.

The season of bitterness and disappointment is what we are to cross over from. One way of entering into the delight of the Lord is to find our place of 'worship.' Naomi was bitter from life's disappointments. Yet waiting for her was the promise of Hope found in a baby in the arms of her Moabite daughter in-law. So, the book of Ruth is not just about Ruth, but it is Naomi's story as well. In addition, it is Boaz's story which foreshadows the events of Jesus Christ as our Kinsman Redeemer.

---

50 http://www.webstersdictionary1828.com/Dictionary/vision
51 http://www.webstersdictionary1828.com/Dictionary/Omnipresence

Our Kinsman Redeemer reaches out to every one of us in the story line of our lives.

In Ruth 4, we read about the birth of Obed, Naomi's grandson through Boaz and Ruth.

Obed means worshipper.

We are restored into 'delight and pleasantness' through 'worship' of God. We are delivered from arrogance and bitterness —these things blocked our view of God's vision. When we are focused on our disappointment, we can become bitter. However, when we come to the Lord with thanksgiving, praise, and worship, He heals and restores us.

Truly in His presence is fullness of joy.[52]

God is not as concerned about us being happy as He is about us being obedient to His will. His process leads us through our 'not so happy' moments. This is where the sacrifice of praise is worked out in our lives. When we do not feel like singing praises, by letting our broken praise come forth through the tears anyway, this is an act of sacrificial praise.

In *Unshakeable Hope* by Derek Prince, he writes:

> God is more concerned for you and me to be "good' than "happy"… If at any time it is necessary for me to be unhappy that it may produce goodness in me, then God will always go for goodness—and sacrifice temporarily the happiness…[53]

---

[52] You will make known to me the way **of** life; In Your **presence** is **fullness of joy**; In Your right hand there are pleasures forever. Psalm 16:11 NASB

[53] Prince, Derek, *Unshakable Hope* by Derek Prince (Destiny Image, 2019).

The Lord is singing over us His breakthrough song and saying of His Bride.

"My delight is in her."

Perhaps when we lean into His song, we will turn from bitterness to delight.

The valley of the Covid-19 pandemic isolation, our sudden upheaval and return move to Utah, brought me to a choice. My landscape changed again. My view no longer a dream fulfilled, but the debris of my dead dream. There was a huge 'Y' in front of me. I could have remained in California and Randy move to Utah until he retired. Yet I felt the Father drawing me to prefer and honor my husband. I did not know this path would be strewn with loneliness, lost vision, and emotions I had to face in order to remain sweet and not become bitter. The path was strewn with questions and unknowns. Happiness was fleeting. Brief bouts with utter despair in the midst of processing disappointment plagued me. It was an unexpected 'dark night of the soul.'

Trusting God—trust in God produced new Hope.

Hope is powerful.

Hope is healing.

Hope turns our lives into prayers, which release a healing flow to us and through us. Hope fuels faith to believe, *God works all things for good for those who love Him and are called…*[54]

---

[54] See Romans 8:28

A Divine RE– The More Excellent Way

As you listen to me, my beloved child, you will grow in wisdom and your heart will be drawn into understanding, which will empower you to make right decisions.[55]

---
55 Proverbs 23:19 TPT

25

WISDOM SPEAKS

Wisdom Calling

Can't you hear the voice of Wisdom?
From the top of the mountains of influence
she speaks into the gateways of the glorious city.
At the place where pathways merge,
at the entrance of every portal,
there she stands, ready to impart understanding,
shouting aloud to all who enter,
preaching her sermon to those who will listen.[56]

Wisdom speaks at the gates.

Wisdom invites us to encounter the Lord so we don't miss His appearing at the End of the Age.

Wisdom invites us to get fresh oil for our lampstands.

Wisdom releases transformation. Transformation comes through encounter.

Wisdom is inviting. It is the King's invitation.

> Step-away from man's wisdom.
> Step-out of human reasoning.

---

56 Proverbs 8:1-3 TPT

Pass through the gateway—the open door. Come up to wisdom's ways.
God's ways are higher—wiser—pure—filled with delight in truth—making free—empowering to endure and take up your cross.
To walk with the uncaused One who is Love; Yahweh Ahava.

To love and pray for haters.
To lay down one's life for God's friends and pray for His enemies.
This is The Cruciform Life.

Blueprints are found in wisdom and revelation.

Resources for heaven's will—Wisdom funds His plans.
Wisdom is a well of resource.
Seek the Lord while He may be found.
Ascend the mountain of the Lord and bring back what He gives.
From heaven's perspective, speak it into the earth.
Written and spoken Word.
AMEN!

For the Lord gives wisdom;
From His mouth come knowledge and understanding.
He stores up sound wisdom for the upright;
He is a shield to those who walk in integrity,
Guarding the paths of justice,
And He preserves the way of His godly ones.
Then you will discern righteousness and justice
And equity and every good course.

For wisdom will enter your heart
And knowledge will be pleasant to your soul;

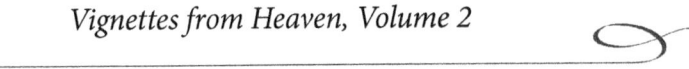

Discretion will guard you,
Understanding will watch over you...[57]

There is a gate to the hidden garden of our hearts.
When we let Wisdom speak,
the Word of Wisdom enters our hearts.

---

57 Proverbs 2:6-11 NASB

My Reflections

26

WHEN DREAMS DIE

The dream had lingered in the distance,
Year after year
It seemed it would never appear.

Then suddenly another dream
Confirmed the dream was near.

The dream came,
I could not doubt
Even when it seemed hard to believe.

For the dream was as real as the sand beneath my feet,
As tangible as oceans waves crashing on the shore.

So long it had tarried,
Then suddenly it came.
But it was not to last
Nor forever remain.
Upheaval removed the place for the dream to stand upon.
Yet the dream was real
Though only for a moment
In time it came
And appeared with joy.
Yes, came it did

And now it's gone
Let joy remain.

As the tears of letting go
Say goodbye
Don't stop hoping
Carry the memory of the dream
Deep within my heart and soul
For on the shores of the dream
   Hope heals
      Hope establishes
         Hope was planted deep within.
So once again
I believe
It is time for another dream[58]

---

[58] April 22, 2020

27

HOPE AWAKENED

Grief is a very strange companion. No one knows how long grief will visit. Grief has to be processed. And when grief lifts, joy really does come.

Weeping endures for a night, but joy comes in the morning.[59]

I was stunned by the back-to-back seasons of grief. I really thought I would be good with each change. Alas, it was not so. Change is a unique path to navigate. Moving into a dream was much easier. Losing the dream took me on a journey of not losing hope.

I am thankful the Lord did not leave me alone even though there were times I did not feel His nearness. His presence seemed absent in the losing of my dream. In the midst of this, I knew He was carrying me. At times doubt obscured His love, but His love never failed nor left me. I know the prayers of others carried me as well. He carried me on His Word. He continues to carry me, and He will carry you, beloved.

He is faithful.

I am thankful.
I am hopeful.
I am joyful.

Hope leads us to find the path through grief and into the land of living fully awakened.

---

59 See Psalm 30:5

A Divine RE- The More Excellent Way

My Reflections

28

SATISFY THE WEARY

For I will [fully] satisfy the weary soul, and I will replenish every languishing and sorrowful person. ⁶⁰

The Lord created the earth and all in it for our pleasure. The enemy looked and was jealous. So, the serpent deceived us into eating from the wrong tree.

We lose the wonder and beauty of being with God in His garden when we eat from the Tree of Knowledge of Good and Evil. The enemy deceived humanity and we lost the wonder of ALL God created.

Sometimes it's the hard seasons, which cause us to slow down. Grief, loss, and sorrow can be special places to meet with God.

We cannot deny our humanness, our humanity. Even Jesus was acquainted with grief and sorrow.

He was despised and forsaken of men, a man of sorrows and acquainted with grief; and like one from whom men hide their face He was despised and we did not esteem Him. ⁶¹

---

60 Jeremiah 31:25 AMPC
61 Isaiah 53:3 NASB

 *A Divine RE– The More Excellent Way*

> *My soul weeps because of grief; strengthen me according to Your word.* [62]

We can lean on the One who came to restore to us the joy of salvation. To bring us back to the garden.

We can bring our tears to the One who cried tears of anguish.

We can bring our pain to the One who endured suffering.

He will restore us and bring us to His Oasis of Peace as Psalm 23 in *The Passion Translation* describes the process of walking with our Shepherd through dark valleys.

> *Yahweh is my best friend and my shepherd.*
> *I always have more than enough.*
> *He offers a resting place for me in his luxurious love.*
> *His tracks take me to an oasis of peace near the quiet brook of bliss.*
> *That's where He restores and revives my life.*
> *He opens before me the right path*
> *and leads me along in his footsteps of righteousness*
> *so that I can bring honor to his name.*
> *Even when your path takes me through*
> *the valley of deepest darkness,*
> *fear will never conquer me, for you already have!*
> *Your authority is my strength and my peace.*
> *The comfort of your love takes away my fear.*
> *I'll never be lonely, for you are near.*
> *You become my delicious feast*
> *even when my enemies dare to fight.*

---

62 Psalm 111:28 NASB

You anoint me with the fragrance of your Holy Spirit;
you give me all I can drink of you until my cup overflows.
So why would I fear the future?
Only goodness and tender love pursue me all the days of my life.
Then afterward, when my life is through,
I'll return to your glorious presence to be forever with you! [63]

Grief can drag us right into a pit of weariness. Yet, if we invite Jesus into our grief, He will lead us through and help us heal.

---

63 Psalm 23 TPT

My Reflections

29

GRIEF

I had no idea
How dark the grip
Upon my heart.
"Would it be
 So much less?"
I thought.
But now I feel
This awful loss.
A pain my tears
Have yet to ease.
I want to look
But I know,
You are not where
You used to be.
So, I must
Look in my heart
And pray for eyes to see.

Dear Jesus,

You are my best friend. You are everything I need. You are familiar with grief and sorrow. You always lead me. Knowing you is having you right here, right now. In you I have more than enough.

Please help me to grieve well as I release the sorrow and grief to you. Help me to help others who are grieving as well. Help me to see, to know, and discern your way and your thoughts on how to process loss.

Give me a glimpse of hope, eyes of faith, a trusting heart, and peace that passes all understanding.

Jesus, You are wonderful.

Abba, You are a good Father.

Holy Spirit, I receive Your comfort.

30

TRANSITION OF THE LORD

The transition of the Lord is a journey from one way of seeing and doing, into the next way He desires us to walk with Him. Maturity happens through the process of growing and changing.

Transition out of seasons of trauma, pain, betrayal, and brokenness invites the posture of humility to deal with the tares of our souls. Years ago I read *The Thrones of Our Souls* by Paul Keith Davis. It is a powerful revelation of the Lord dealing with the places in our souls that are ruled by the dark side. I clearly remember the process of inviting the Lord into every place of my life. Little did I know it would be a life-long journey becoming and remaining free from strongholds. For the enemy of our souls uses the pain, trauma, and betrayal to sow fresh seeds of tares into the soil of our hearts. These bitter worm-wood seeds come from the brokenness of humanity.

As we cross through the valley of darkest night and deepest shadows, the Lord will invite us to streams of His Living Word where we are cleansed. The cleansing removes the residue of lies where tares have grown.

If someone brings out the worst in us, then there still is the worst in us. The 'worst' is what our Father is after. He wants to Re-place it with Jesus' best:

Re-place the 'worst" with:

His Word

His Life

His Light

His Love

James 1:21 is a powerful instruction from the Lord. This instruction follows after James' exhortation earlier in this chapter to ask for wisdom. The Lord will give generously. Note, every good and perfect gift comes from our Father. What a powerful chapter of goodness from our Father's heart. We are called to surrender to the process of releasing what hinders love. It is being filled with every aspect of love, which transforms us by the power of Holy Spirit. What a wonderful exchange. I have included both the *New American Standard* and *The Passion Translation* here for consideration.

> *Therefore, putting aside all filthiness and all that remains of wickedness, in humility receive the word implanted, which is able to save your souls.*[64]

> *So this is why we abandon everything morally impure and all forms of wicked conduct. Instead, with a sensitive spirit we absorb God's Word, which has been implanted within our nature, for the Word of Life has power to continually deliver us.*[65]

Larry Randolph shared a powerful truth in regard to how the Lord instructed him to see others' issues. They are to be looked upon as weaknesses and not faults. Faultfinding causes us to become critical

---

64 James 1:21 NASB
65 James 1:21 TPT

and judgmental. When we do this, we are of no use to a loving Father who desires to fill our words and actions with His love. When we see weaknesses, we can be assured we all have them. Invite Jesus and the power of His overcoming blood into these places.

How we see will determine how we respond. We need the Lord's lenses, His Omni Vision.

When we cross over from dead thoughts and thieving beliefs, we enter the land of the living.

> *I would have despaired unless I had believed that I*
> *would see the goodness of the Lord*
> *In the land of the living.*
> *Wait for the Lord;*
> *Be strong and let your heart take courage;*
> *Yes, wait for the Lord.*[66]

This is where Hope is.

    This is where promises burst forth.

        This is where favor and blessing carry us through.

In this world Jesus told us we would have troubles. He also told us we would overcome. This is the overcomer's journey. This life gives us many opportunities to learn about forgiveness, grace, overcoming, and so many other divine RE- lessons in transition.

Transformation is happening in transition. Holy Spirit has us on a process journey. On this path, we must remember:

    God is good—His goodness abounds—His love endures.

    In every season we are blessed because we are His.

---

66 Psalm 27:13-14

My Reflections

31

JESUS, YOU'RE ENOUGH

When I am alone
In change and transition,
When grief and sorrow
Grip my heart,
Help me to know–

Jesus, You're enough.

When I feel I have failed
And am picking up the pieces,
Trying hard to fit the mold
Assure me to know–

Jesus, You're enough.

When Hope seems to have
Walked out the door,
And dark despair wants to fill the void,
Help me see you standing near
That I may know–

Jesus, You're enough.

When comparison measures me
And I fall short,
Let me see the scales of love.
Balance me to know–

Jesus, You're enough.

When fear of man taunts my soul
Expecting me to perform,
I choose to look to You,
Cast the burden at Your feet,
Finding rest as I learn to trust—

Jesus, You're enough.

When my eyes You open
To see Your plan and dream for my life,
Knowing it's so much more than I can do,
I put my hope in You,
Surrender now for I believe—

Jesus, You're enough.

And when my days
Near the end,
With assurance and hope
I look up to see,
My welcome home

Jesus, You're enough.

32

RENEW YOUR MIND

Renew your mind.

Re-wire in Faith,

    Re-wire in God's Truth,

        Re-wire in Believing God

            Re-wire in seeing His best in everything.

Don't set the affections of your heart on this world or in loving the things of the world. The love of the Father and the love of the world are incompatible. For all that the world can offer us— the gratification of our flesh, the allurement of the things of the world, and the obsession with status and importance —none of these things come from the Father but from the world. This world and its desires are in the process of passing away, but those who love to do the will of God live forever.[67]

Our thoughts and what we focus on can keep us in negative life cycles. We have an inheritance to live in this world as Jesus is renewing our mind with His Divine thoughts and ways. As He does so, He will RE-calibrate us. When we RE-new our minds with faith, hope, and love, transformation happens. The meaning of

---

67 1 John 2:15-17 TPT

 *A Divine RE– The More Excellent Way*

transformation from the 1828 Webster's Dictionary defines what the power of Holy Spirit does. When we partner with process instead of struggling against His ways, we transcend into transformation.

- The change of the soul into a divine substance,
- In theology, a change of heart in man, by which his disposition and temper are conformed to the divine image; a change from enmity to holiness and love.[68]

Studies reveal we can change habits in 21 days. Dr. Carolyn Leaf has a 21-Day Brain Detox program many have found very helpful to renew their minds.

Our souls are where the heart, will, and emotions flow. Transformation in our hearts renews our minds in Christ Jesus.

Stop imitating the ideals and opinions of the culture around you, but be inwardly transformed by the Holy Spirit through a total reformation of how you think. This will empower you to discern God's will as you live a beautiful life, satisfying and perfect in his eyes.[69]

---

68 Webster's 1828 Dictionary online; http://www.webstersdictionary1828.com/Dictionary/transformation
69 Romans 12:2 TPT

33

YOUR MOUTH —A WOMB OR A TOMB?

Racham: The Hebrew word for "compassion" (*racham*) means "to love deeply, like a mother's love." *Racham* is a homonym for "womb," with an implication that God's love is like the love of a mother carrying a child in her womb.

We can shape culture with our words. How are we impacting our culture? Are our mouths a womb or a tomb? What are we creating with our words?

> *For we did not receive the spirit of this world system but the Spirit of God, so that we might come to understand and experience all that grace has lavished upon us. And we articulate these realities with the words imparted to us by the Spirit and not with the words taught by human wisdom. We join together Spirit-revealed truths with Spirit-revealed words. Someone living on an entirely human level rejects the revelations of God's Spirit, for they make no sense to him. He can't understand the revelations of the Spirit because they are only discovered by the illumination of the Spirit. Those who live in the Spirit are able to carefully evaluate all things, and they are subject to the scrutiny of no one but God. For Who has ever*

intimately known the mind of the Lord Yahweh well enough to become his counselor?
Christ has, and we possess Christ's perceptions.[70]

Our words come from our thoughts. What we watch, read, listen to, and give focus to forms our thoughts.

We need the Spirit of Christ to help us. The fullness of the Spirit of the Lord:

> Spirit of wisdom and understanding
> Spirit of counsel and might
> Spirit of knowledge and the fear of the Lord [71]

In *The Passion Translation*, Isaiah 11:2-5 gives a very descriptive word of the Seven-fold Spirit of God enabling us to grasp the meaning of His fullness.

> *...the Spirit of Yahweh will rest upon him,*
> *the Spirit of Extraordinary Wisdom,*
> *the Spirit of Perfect Understanding*
> *the Spirit of Wise Strategy,*
> *the Spirit of Mighty Power,*
> *the Spirit of Revelation,*
> *and the Spirit of the Fear of Yahweh.*
>
> *He will find his delight in living*
> *by the Spirit of the Fear of the Lord.*
> *He will neither judge by appearances*
> *nor make his decisions based on rumors.*
> *With righteousness he will uphold justice for the poor*
> *and defend the lowly of the earth.*

---

70 1 Corinthians 2:12-16 TPT
71 See Isaiah 11:2

> *His words will be like a scepter of power*
> *that conquers the world,*
> *and with his breath he will slay the lawless one.*
> *Righteousness will be his warrior's sash*
> *and faithfulness his belt.*[72]

The Spirit of the Lord, the mind of Christ, the fullness of God in Christ...we have all received of His fullness.[73]

RE-New; a renewed mind, renewal through the Spirit of Christ transforms us.

It is true repentance; a turning upside down to be made upside right in Christ.

> *O God, my saving God,*
> *deliver me fully from every sin,*
> *even the sin that brought bloodguilt.*
> *Then my heart will once again be thrilled to sing*
> *the passionate songs of joy and deliverance!*
> *Lord God, unlock my heart, unlock my lips,*
> *and I will overcome with my joyous praise!*
> *For the source of your pleasure is not in my performance*
> *or the sacrifices I might offer to you.*[74]

Transformation, being RE-new (renewed) growing in our union with Christ.

> *Through our union with Christ we too have been claimed by God as his own inheritance. Before we were even born, he gave us our destiny; that we would fulfill the plan of God who always accomplishes every purpose and plan in his heart.*[75]

---
72 Isaiah 11:2-5 TPT
73 John 1:16; of His fullness we have all received.
74 Psalm 51:14-16 TPT
75 Ephesians 1:11 TPT

A Divine RE- The More Excellent Way

My Reflections

34

RE- TURN

Return to the House of Prayer Way

*'I will welcome you into my holy mountain and make you joyful in my **house of prayer**. I will accept every sacrifice and **off**ering that you place on my altar, for my **house of worship** will be known as a **house of prayer** for all people.'*[76]

Return to the House of Prayer Way.

My way—not your way

My way—not man's way

Return to Yahweh! [77]

Lift up your eyes to the heavenly realm... [78]

Look up! This is an invitation to see heaven's pattern. This invitation has been extended to us. Some hear. Others need awakened ears to hear.

About ten years ago, I remember sitting in my quiet time before a leaders' gathering. I heard the sound of a resounding clock tower;

---

[76] Isaiah 56:7 TPT
[77] July 9, 2019
[78] Isaiah 51:6

the sound made me shake. The Lord said to pick up my pen and write. What I saw and heard shook me.

I saw the Lord's mighty right hand sweep across tall structures and lay them flat. He spoke to me a time was coming where what man had built would not stand. Only what His people built according to His ways, His plans, His heart with prayer at the front would remain.

It was sobering, and it was awakening. It is His Kingdom coming.

*He rebuked them, saying, "The Scriptures declare, 'My **Father's house** is to be filled with **prayer—a house of prayer**, not a cave of bandits!'"[79]*

---

79 Luke 19:46 TPT

35

LOST IN THE RACE

I felt lost in a race, in a race I couldn't win. Much like Timothy, our childhood pet hamster. Timothy had a wheel in his cage. He would run, run, run never getting anywhere. His little feet on the wheel going fast, expending pent-up energy and producing nothing. This scene in my memory came back to me, and I thought all he had to do was jump off. And he would do so. The little guy would often escape the confines of his cage. One day he was found drowned in our above ground pool. No more running.

Somehow this hopeless memory imprinted me. Timothy was never really free. Many of us never find the freedom of living fully alive in God. We must awaken to the truth God came and rescued us from the never-ending rat race.

In this Divine RE- He is awakening His church, His people, His Bride to the reality of the rhythm of living life from His heart. He told us in Proverbs 4:23 to above all guard the affections of our heart for from it flow the springs…the very issues…the life we live from. (Paraphrased)

In this season, A Divine RE-, I have encountered the fountain of grace in Christ Jesus. He is empowering hope.

Revelation from glory to glory, with its 'In Between' place is where the process of story forms. Life is story. We go through tests of the heart. Humbling yourself, repenting, and turning from self-focus are necessary steps. Turning away from complaining and bad attitudes are essential steps. We can choose to allow truth to cleanse our souls and align in heart towards God with humility.

Pride had polluted the river flowing from my own heart. Pride had me think way too highly of myself. Pride, wounds, betrayal all led me to the bitter waters of anger, retreat, and withdrawal.

Repentance, an act of humility, leads to grace. God resists the proud, yet fully releases grace to the humble. I chose to Re-discover James 4:6-10.

I love the heights of God—it's the unknowns where my weakness is very evident. He tells us in 2 Corinthians 12:9:

> *My grace is always more than enough for you, and my power finds it's full expression through your weakness. (TPT)*

When we receive His grace in difficult and uncertain times, we discover His grace is more than sufficient.

> Grace, grace to heal our bodies.
> Grace, grace to keep moving forward.
> Grace, grace to believe God.

It is in His grace we discover His great faithfulness. He is the one who perfects us. I will never forget the day He said to me; "Tracee Anne, I do not expect you to be perfect, I perfect you".

That is freedom! This is a total Divine RE- from what has been expected. A spirit of excellence is very different than a heavy yoke of perfection. One is from the Tree of Life, the other is the Tree of Knowledge of Good and evil. One releases the rhythm of grace, the other the ugly taskmaster of performance.

> *Since you are children of a perfect Father in heaven, you are to be perfect like Him.*[80]

The footnote in *The Passion Translation* for this verse is astounding:

> The Greek and Aramaic words for "perfect" can also mean "whole"; complete, fully mature, lacking nothing, all-inclusive and well-rounded.

What a powerful RE- Moment (realization).

The Lord is awakening us to our infinite need of Him. It is Him— He helps—He perfects.

Our weakness He fills with Himself.

When we surrender, it gives Him access—entry to make us whole.

Our Father perfects us. Our Father makes us whole.

Make it personal: *My Father perfects me, My Father makes me whole.*

He perfects us. His DNA—Divine Nature Applied to our lives makes us whole. His blood and His glory make us whole.

Wisdom introduced me to a revelation about spiritual TNT. TNT, standing for Total Nucleus Transformation, makes us new.

His Total Nucleus Transformation through His Holy Spirit makes us new. He fulfills us. He is fully alive; therefore, we are fully alive in Him. Let Him have full possession of you—surrender!

---

[80] Matthew 5:48 TPT

Divine union and communion happen as we humble ourselves and yield to Him. This is falling upon the Rock, Christ Jesus. Our Father is very good. Let our hearts be full of His joy.

36

LEANING

Leaning
   Learning
Abiding
   Arising
Safe
   Secure
Trusting
   Together
Standing
   Strengthened
Loving
   Leaning

Jesus is the Center
   He is my peace
      He is my all

Pride is a devil
   It removes me
      From grace

Humility is a gift
   A gateway to grace

All that I am
   I am in Christ
For what I think
   I am
I should not
   Without Him
I am nothing

As I surrender in humility
   I find Him.

In "I Am"
   Christ manifested
I am fully everything
   He created me to be

37

UNRAVEL THE MOTIVES

I asked the Lord about the "Y" in the road of the Divine RE-.

My question was directed towards those of us called to be His leaders.

I heard:

> The difference between leaders today and the heroes of faith from history can be summed up as follows:
>
>> Those who followed after Me were not looking for fame or to be known.
>> They desired to 'obey' above all else.
>> They were not enamored by 'hero' status or being 'somebody'.
>> They desired to know Christ and make Him known.

Look at the disciples, the early church fathers, and the history of martyrs. Those we esteem from church history would probably shudder at the pedestals we have built for them.

> Only Jesus be lifted up!

UNRAVEL THE MOTIVES

My Reflections

38

RE-TURN TO SON-SHIP

I heard my Love speak clearly:

Be careful—Pray the accusations in the body do not become the Salem witch-hunts—

Fault-Finding

I have stood in front of the anointed, concerned by their unhealed wounds. There are those in ministry who shared they were told to not discuss or let anyone know of their personal or relational struggles. The 'pull up your bootstraps, put on the mask, dance the dance, and sing the song' performance Christianity platform. Abraham and Sarah used Hagar to birth what they wanted. They then tossed her aside along with the child she birthed.

I have gone with warnings to precious ones to slow down, get healed, be with Jesus, and let Him do the work. Some heard the word and sought the Lord. They are still standing with Christ in ministry. Others have had very public failures, leaving many wounded, and they, themselves, devastated as well. God wants us to remember healing, reconciliation, and restoration are available for all. Galatians 6:1 tells us we are called to "restore such a one".

 A Divine RE- The More Excellent Way

> *Brethren, even if anyone is caught in any trespass, you who are spiritual, restore such a one in a spirit of gentleness; each one looking to yourself, so that you too will not be tempted.*[81]

The exhortation is to do so in a spirit of gentleness. We are not to be critical lest you be tempted. I thank God I have seen many leaders operate in a spirit of gentleness restoring fallen ones. No one is perfect. Not one of us is without failure.

Awe at the lure of power fills every mountain of society. The religion mountain has long struggled with battling the demons of pride, fear of man, insecurity, desire to be known, etc. Some struggle with 'not good enough' When favor and attention draw them to the front before their time, the soil of the garden of their heart has not been properly prepared to carry the weight of being somebody known.

Perhaps platforms are manmade thrones where souls of men are drawn into the drama of ministry instead of the mystery of Christ.

I could have been one of these casualties. But the Lord spoke very strongly to me when I was a young follower of Jesus. He put before me a choice: You can birth Ishmael or Isaac. I was being released into platform ministry in the early years of knowing Christ. Power gifts flowed and the Lord moved mightily. I moved with Holy Spirit in the word of knowledge and prophecy without even knowing much about the gifts of the Spirit.

The Lord revealed to me if I continued on this path of ministry, I would be a shooting star without longevity. He gave me a

---

81 Galatians 6:1 NASB

choice—Ishmael or Isaac. His way or man's way. He then invited me into a season of discipleship, healing, and deliverance. It has been a fascinating adventure.

I was summoned into hiddenness in Christ. We all are invited to this place. His call: "Come follow Me, take up your cross, and I will show you the more excellent way". It is a path laden with the mystery of surrender, dying to self, and freedom. There is great joy because Jesus becomes our reward. It is filled with beauty and brokenness: the beauty of God shining forth from the brokenness of our humanity.

Since the Lord commissioned me into ministry, I have seen Him do marvelous wonders. I have experienced God in His astounding ways. I've seen miracles, healing, and deliverances as He filled me and worked through me. His glory has come into gatherings. People encounter the Lord and are transformed.

The Lord is to be the One on the Throne of platform ministry. I have shared if you put me on a pedestal (throne), the Lord will knock me off in front of you. Transparency became the seat I sit upon. Transparency comes from humbling and yielding to the Lord. Humility makes way for the Lord of glory and His Kingdom to manifest. Transparency is the place where in my weakness, the beauty and glory of God is seen. It is not my strength or gifts, but His that heal and touch people.

There are those who make way for God to be glorified and magnified. They have allowed the works of Christ to be made real in their lives. I've seen the glory of the Lord come into a room when one of His own gives way for Him to move. When Jesus is lifted up, people come to Him.

A Divine RE– The More Excellent Way

Jesus leads us to Our Father. He made a way for Holy Spirit, our helper, to come and clothe us with the ability to live a morally excellent life. Relationship with Our Father, His Son, and Holy Spirit bring us into A Divine RE; The More Excellent Way. Love flows in us and through us. People encounter Jesus and are forever changed.

RE-turn to Sonship.

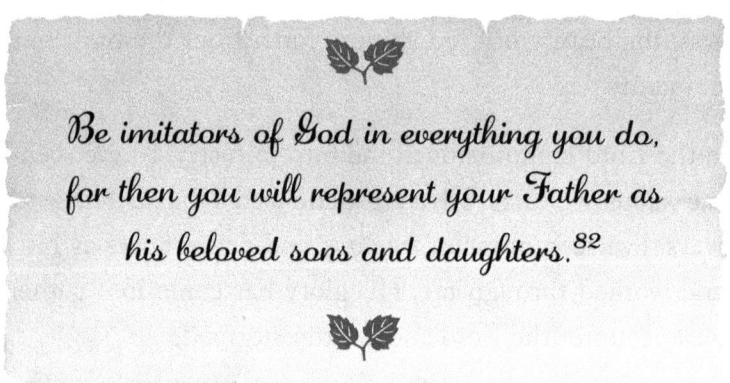

Be imitators of God in everything you do, for then you will represent your Father as his beloved sons and daughters.[82]

When we discover Christ's invitation to Holy rest and transformation, we will discover the rhythm of grace.

We are learning to navigate new waters. We need the Light of Christ to illuminate the eyes of our hearts to remain on His path.

---

82 Ephesians 5:1 TPT

39

CELEBRATED, NOT TOLERATED: TRUTH OR FAIRY TALE?

There is a saying among Christian circles: "Go *where you are celebrated, not just tolerated.*" Once upon a time I believed this as truth. I chose to go where I was being celebrated, giving God my "yes" and taking up the cross.

I would soon discover the Lord took my "yes" seriously. I quickly learned taking up the cross and laying down your life is not the fairy tale of being celebrated, but the reality of putting on a servant's apron and getting low. It's not going to the head of the table, or (what we see today in a celebrity mindset church) being the next "who's who" on the platform. It is embracing what Jesus endured on the road into Jerusalem, where the crowds shouted *"Hosanna!"* one day and *"Crucify him!"* the next.

While serving a well-known ministry, I was in the hidden place, not out front. I enjoyed this place. It was incredible to sense the amazing presence of God, to see His glory, to receive His heart from heaven (the Kingdom of love) and to release it on earth… But some around me saw the gift of God on my life and felt I should have a more public place.

I heard the words through multiple voices in this season: "Go *where you are celebrated, not just tolerated.*" I took it as a confirmation the Lord was inviting me to the front to be celebrated. I accepted the offer to serve another ministry, whose leaders felt I needed a more public place. They were precious lovers of God. I jumped at the chance to go. It felt like favor had made a way for me.

I desired to serve the Lord. I had made the promise to go wherever He led me. I love Him so much! But this "celebrated" move was not the Lord's place or His positioning. My zeal, mixed with religious duty, produced striving and seeking to be recognized. I wanted to be seen. I had been rejected much, so to have this kind of acceptance and invitation made me feel special and celebrated.

While on one of the organization's amazing ministry trips, the Lord revealed to me a scenario He was going to allow to unfold. He showed me how He would allow the heart of one to turn against me, and this person would go to one of the leaders. This would cause the door of ministering alongside them to close. This was because I was not serving where He had called me.

He had not led me to this position. He instructed me to die to self and go back and serve where He had called me. I wept the tears of one who knew I had gone my own way instead of the way of Love. It all played out as our Father had revealed to me. It was very painful. I was being crucified. His instructions to me were to remain silent and go to the cross.

> *If anyone wishes to come after Me, he must deny himself, and take up his cross daily and follow Me. For whoever wishes to save his life will lose it, but whoever loses his life for My sake, he is the one who will save it. For what is a*

man profited if he gains the whole world, and loses or forfeits himself? [83]

I returned and served the ministry I was called to for many more years. I learned precious truths in serving a humble man of God. And I felt God celebrating me as I found myself in Him.

The same temptation came again where dear ones would see the anointing on my life and want me to go places I was not called to go. I had to war with the temptation of *going to be celebrated once again*.

Yet through it all I experienced great joy. I found the path the Lord has laid out to be filled with wonder and blessing. In the process my Divine Re: I let go of the yoke of religious duty and the need for approval. I took the yoke of Jesus and gave Him the heavy burdens.

The mature children of God are those who are moved by the impulses of the Holy Spirit. And you did not receive the "spirit of religious duty," leading you back into the fear *of never being good enough*. But you have received the "Spirit of full acceptance," enfolding you into the family of God. And you will never feel orphaned, for as he rises up within us, our spirits join him in saying the words of tender affection, "Beloved Father!" For the Holy Spirit makes God's fatherhood real to us as he whispers into our innermost being, "You are God's beloved child!"[84]

I found my place as a loved daughter; my position in His heart first. Everything else flowed from abiding where He placed me and led me.

---

83 Luke 9:23-25 NASB
84 Romans 8:14-16 TPT

 *A Divine RE- The More Excellent Way*

I have discovered the statement "G*o where you are celebrated, not just tolerated."* has left many feeling like outcasts. They go from place to place looking to be celebrated by man. They see certain ones promoted and their own gifts left unopened. They wander to the next place feeling forsaken and forgotten.

Unfortunately, this kind of culture leaves people feeling rejected because of an unholy expectation. This feeds the enemy's tactic to keep the sons and daughters of God orphans. The orphan mentality restrains us from receiving His love. This prevents us from drawing near to the Lord and each other. The progression of rejection pushes many into isolation,

Too often we only celebrate the highlighted ones. Yet the Father celebrates all His children. He desires to pour out His Spirit on all flesh. The Spirit empowers us to live a life of power and freedom from the enemy. The Spirit in us cries out the truth of our identity as sons and daughters.

> *Yet all of this was so that he would redeem and set free all those held hostage to the written law so that we would receive our freedom and a full legal adoption as his children. And so that we would know for sure that we are his true children, God released the Spirit of Sonship into our hearts—moving us to cry out intimately, "My Father! You're our true Father!" Now we're no longer living like slaves under the law, but we enjoy being God's very own sons and daughters! And because we're his, we can access everything our Father has—for we are heirs of God through Jesus, the Messiah!*[85]

---

85 Galatians 4:5-7 TPT

When we learn to abide in Him and only do what He asks of us, we find the joy of being loved and secure children of God. Discerning the Father's heart and path for us is key. It is not to tolerate the fairy tales of man, but to know the truth of being sons and daughters of God. The love of our Father grounds us, bringing us into stability. When we know our identity in Him, we can lead others to Him—our good, good Father.

Flee the fairy tale and RE-turn to Truth!

Awake:
> Awake to Christ in you, the HOPE of glory!

Aware:
> Aware of His nature and life living in you and through you!

Alert:
> Alert to His movements, intents, divine guidance, and Shamar protection![86]

---

[86] Shamar: Hebrew word meaning to keep, to watch, to protect

40

TURNING POINT

While walking Shiloh, my dog, on a beautiful summer day, I was praying in the Spirit. All of sudden the word 'Kahana' kept coming forth with other unknown tongues. Then 'mahalo' came forth which I knew was Hawaiian. When I got home, I researched meanings for both.

Kahana in Hawaiian means:

> Turning point
> Wild wind common in Kahana

Mahalo means:

> Thanks, gratitude, admiration, praise, esteem, regards or respects

As I wrote these words which had come forth on my prayer walk, I felt a wind on the back of my head, and then it encircled me. I heard this phrase:

Holiness is wholeness.

Then I heard:

Turning Point

 A Divine RE- The More Excellent Way

I believe the Lord was revealing His *Turning Point Winds* are coming as we praise Him with thankful hearts. Gratitude and honor unto the Lord bring us into His holiness, which is wholeness. This is the Turning Point.

"The Turning Point"
A "Flowetic" Word

In the Turning Point we are invited
To posture our hearts in
Gratitude and thankfulness unto The Lord.
Reverential Awe of The Lord-
Releases the winds of
"The Turning Point"

Humility and brokenness over weakness and failures
Bring us into His healing presence.

Jesus Christ binds us up and makes us whole.

Happy Holiness brings us into wholeness
Wholeness empowers us to live in Christ's fullness.

Whether weeping or abounding
In enduring or enjoying
In every season
The Lord is above it all
And we are seated with Him.

The joy of the Lord
Is a quiet calm in troubled times and a source of gladness.

I know what it means to lack, and I know what it means to experience overwhelming abundance. For I'm trained in the secret of overcoming all things, whether in fullness or in hunger. And I find that the strength of Christ's explosive power infuses me to conquer every difficulty.[87]

Resilience is key to endurance, which produces the ability to flourish.

Yahweh wants us to flourish.

It comes through the pathway of tears, suffering, and

> OVERCOMING.

Joy – a quiet calm

Come out of the fog

> You are overcoming complacency to Live RE- new and fully alive!

A Divine RE-; as many have called a RE-set. Which way will you RE-set? To God's way of hope, joy, faith and delight, living in truth and light?

Or will you linger on cliff's edge of despair and fear under the dark cloud?

No!

You are called to come up here and sit with Christ in the realms of Divine Love where faith flourishes, HOPE Overcomes and God's Presence Empowers you to live from victory's rest.

---

[87] Philippians 4:12-13 TPT

 *A Divine RE– The More Excellent Way*

Until then, there are three things that remain: faith, hope, and love—yet love surpasses them all. So above all else, let love be the beautiful prize for which you run.[88]

Your faith and love rise within you as you access all the treasures of your inheritance stored up in the heavenly realm. For the revelation of the true gospel is as real today as the day you first heard of our glorious hope, now that you have believed in the truth of the gospel.[89]

For we remember before our God and Father how you put your faith into practice, how your love motivates you to serve others, and how unrelenting is your hope-filled patience in our Lord Jesus Christ.[90]

Thankfulness and awe of the Lord work together.

When we see Him as who He is, not just what He does, our hearts awaken to move with His turning in His timing. What He does flows from His essence, the nature and character of His awesomeness. As we turn towards seeing Him do what only He can do, let it awaken the goodness of who He is as the Door of Hope.

From our position in Him, we do what we are RE- Born to do.

The goodness of God is revealed over and over through His power to overturn, to save, to deliver.

What grace and glory.

---

[88] 1 Corinthians 13:13 TPT
[89] Colossians 1:5 TPT
[90] 1 Thessalonians 1:3 TPT

To be undone by the awe of the Eternal, All-sufficient One who is worthy.

1 Thessalonians 5:8 exhorts us:

But since we belong to the day, we must stay alert and clear-headed by placing the breastplate of faith and love over our hearts, and a helmet of the hope of salvation over our thoughts.

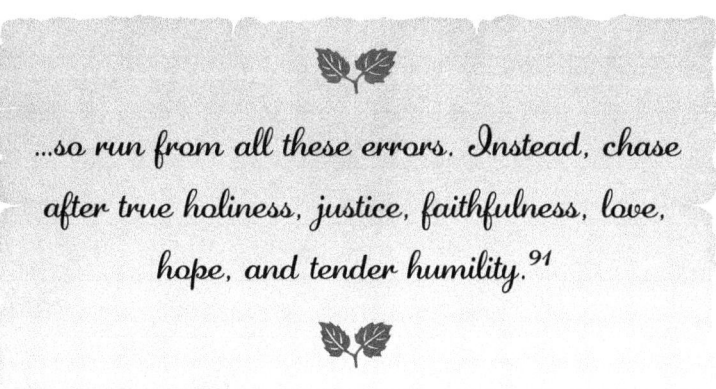

...so run from all these errors. Instead, chase after true holiness, justice, faithfulness, love, hope, and tender humility.[91]

The Turning Point is Now!

---

91 1 Timothy 6:11 TPT

A Divine RE– The More Excellent Way

My Reflections

41

SUNDAY OF ALL SUNDAYS

On September 20, 2020, I heard the Lord say as I awoke:

"It's the Sunday of all Sundays."

I felt anticipation and expectancy in my spirit. Yet I pondered and wondered what this meant. *Lord, what are you saying?*

Next, the Lord reminded me about the "In Between" he had spoken to me during Good Friday the preceding Passover season.

He said to me,

"'Now it is time to write the 'It Is Finished';
Resurrection HOPE;
The Sunday of all Sundays."

The Sunday of All Sundays

The Word of God promises
The Son of Righteousness
Would rise with healing in His wings

And on that Sunday
The Sunday of all Sundays
After the horror of death
The terror of isolation

A Divine RE- The More Excellent Way

The silent pause
Death seemed to have won

The suffering and anguish
Were about to fly away
On winds of Hope
As wings of resurrection
Power raised the
Son of Righteousness
From the grave

"Where is He?" they pondered.
"What about his promises? "
They lamented.

In the dark night
Of the soul of failing emotions
Doubt and betrayal
Running and hiding

Wings of resurrection
Angels rolling back the stone
As Holy Spirit breath and life
Raised the Risen King .
The Sunday of all Sundays
Forever points the way
To follow the Light
Who is the Life
Whose victory has
Seized the Day!
The cry of hope
"It Is Finished"
Still empties graves of hopelessness today

42

RHYTHMS OF GRACE

Rhythms of Grace are sustaining me,
The kindness of God is keeping all things.
His heart
His love
    His prayers—Yes, Jesus' prayers.
He ever lives to make intercession.
Great is His faithfulness.
Even when circumstances baffle—
Even when life doesn't make sense
Even when my emotions are raging and roaring
    Tossing and turning,
He is the hand that steadies me.
He is the hope holding me.
He is always there.
God is good.
    I trust Him.

Who achieved all this and made it happen?
Who guides the destiny of each generation from the first until now?
I am the One!
I am Yahweh, the First,
The unchanging One
Who will be there in the end! [92]

He is the faithful One!

---

92 Isaiah 41:4 TPT

A Divine RE- The More Excellent Way

My Reflections

43

IN-BETWEEN

In-between there is a story
Test of the heart
Humble thyself
Repent
Turn from self-focus
Turn from complaining
Repent from your attitude and let truth cleanse you.

This is a crucial time
Pride had polluted the river from my heart
Pride had led me to think way too highly of myself
Judging
Criticizing
Anger
Retreating
Withdrawal.

In the middle is the forming
The pruning
The dying
The becoming
A lot between only the Lord and me
If only I would embrace Him
Accepting brokenness' invitation to
Discover humility's path of grace.

I realize feeling and experiencing what I have walked through is a gift. Brokenness is a gift—It is the pathway to humility.

Humble hearts are compassionate hearts.

The Lord began speaking to me about the 'in-between' place in 2019. He continues to bring revelation and understanding about the 'in-between place' personally and through others' teachings.

The process requires listening as we wait. In our time of waiting, we discover the journey of process. Process reveals the obstacles and hindrances the Lord desires to remove.

It comes down to this—Wait on the Lord. Listen for His voice. Embrace the process that He lays before you. If you do so, the process will free you from obstacles and hindrances. Then you move forward in victory and humility.

For many, the last few years, even decade, have been the 'in-between' place…a pathway of transition. It is a crucial time of forming. Tests and fiery trials seem to be at every turn. Each test and trial is created to fashion Christ in us if we embrace His will and ways in the process. It takes careful reflection to see with discerning eyes and hear with the ears of a disciple to know the difference between what is sent of God to form us and what is warfare.

It's not too late to embrace the forming. The Master Potter's hands are upon us. His transforming Life works metamorphosis in us. The struggle in metamorphosis is an important part. It forms the new creation. Just look at the process from caterpillar to butterfly. Many have felt stuck, trying to escape. Jesus did not skip the whipping post, the garden, the cross or the tomb. His path of rejection, betrayal, and death lead to the place of resurrection. What looked like the darkest night would break-forth into the Re- *New Day*!

44

THE SILENT PAUSE

In between the darkest day in history
Where Jesus the Christ was crucified
Laid in a tomb
Slain in darkness

Thunder-Shaking!

Sounds of hope deferred
There was a long, silent pause
In the dark stillness
What was not known or seen

Christ the Breaker went to deepest sheol
Defeated death and every curse
Took the keys back from satan's prison
He cancelled every deed to sin's consequences.

For those who will believe
He paid the ransom
For every prisoner of sin
He broke the chains of oppression
And freed every captive from death's eternal flame.
The blood-stained cross displays His love
A tomb now empty His victory
When He arose
Everything changed!!

He defeated every dark power of sin and sickness
Every curse His blood broke its evil power
Once again,
He makes a spectacle of His enemies.
Once again,
Only believe.
Once again,
Hope is Risen!
Once again,
Resurrection power has come to save.

It is in the moments of 'Pause'.

Pausing from pursuit of the man-made race to pursue the ancient path where purpose meets Holy Spirit empowerment.

It is the process of being transformed, receiving new wings to soar on any kind of wind. Whether peaceful winds or adverse winds, wings of transformation burst forth bringing us into the realization we soar with Holy Spirit in the realm of Shalom.

> "Faith anticipates,
>   Hope expects,
>   Divine love intends to bring us into all the good things God has."
>   —Dr. Mark Chironna

45

THE LESSON OF DOLPHINS

A Re-new perspective—eyes open to see heaven's view. The Lord gave Randy and me a gift in the *'in-between'*. Randy's job Re-located us to California. Shortly after we moved to Riverside, his employer informed him he would be working in El Segundo. This was significantly far from our home for daily travel. The gift was the company paid for an apartment or hotel. We were able to find an apartment on the beach in Redondo. It was a dream come true for me. 30-years of longing, and the dream came suddenly. In the midst of Randy's intense work schedule, this little place became a sweet spot for us.

The dolphins came often during our five months at what we lovingly called; the Redondo Condo. One of our neighbors told me in the twelve years they had lived there they had never seen the dolphins come so close to the shore. In my heart I felt their coming close to the shore was a gift from Our Father to delight my weary heart. The way dolphins play and journey in community fascinated me. Watching them filled my heart with the fullness of joy, gratitude, and wonder. They leap above the waves, and the rhythm of their swim movements seems to be easy. Watching them is sheer delight.

These facts about dolphins spoke to my heart:

- Their community is called a school
- They communicate through frequency
- They protect each other.
  - When one is ill or injured the others gather around it to protect it.
  - If there are not enough in their community, more gather from another community to protect the weak.

Community nurtures The More Excellent Way.

46

BEHOLD DELIVERANCE

Yahweh,
Dispel the dark lies
Yahweh,
Your word says the knowledge of Your glory will cover the earth like the water covers the seas.
Your Truth is light chasing darkness far away.
Light of Love come shine down
Your Light dispels the darkness.
It's the frequency of Your Love.

Every drop of Your blood,
Every drop of Your blood is still crying out.
Every drop of Your blood,
Every drop of Your blood is crying out.

It's Your blood
Divine Love frequency
Quenching every sound of fear
Releasing the song of delightful light and love

The song of salvation,
Songs of deliverance
Songs of joy
Hey Sha=Hey Sha=Hey Sha[93]

---

[93] Hey Sha: Behold Deliverance in Hebrew.

 *A Divine RE– The More Excellent Way*

We sing our prayers God
We sing our decrees
Let the sound break the barrier
Let the sound break the barrier of the curse
Your blood and glory cry out.

In unison,
We Your Bride sing out
Hallelujah
AMEN![94]

'As for the promise which I made you when you came out of Egypt, My Spirit is abiding in your midst; do not fear!' For thus says the Lord of hosts, 'Once more in a little while, I am going to shake the heavens and the earth, the sea also and the dry land. I will shake all the nations; and they will come with the wealth of all nations, and I will fill this house with glory,' says the Lord of hosts. 'The silver is Mine and the gold is Mine,' declares the Lord of hosts. 'The latter glory of this house will be greater than the former,' says the Lord of hosts, 'and in this place I will give peace,' declares the Lord of hosts."[95]

The Lord began to speak to my heart:

Hold Steady—the words confirming *Stay Steady*. He spoke this scripture Psalm 94:11:

> The Lord knows the thoughts of man,
> That they are a mere breath.

---

94 On April 3, 2020, from my spirit came this spiritual song
95 Haggai 2:5-9:

Then He spoke Psalm 10:17 and 18:

> *Yahweh, you have heard the desires of the humble*
> *and seen their hopes.*
> *You will hear their cries and encourage their hearts.*
> *The orphans and the oppressed will be terrified no longer,*
> *for you will bring them justice, and no earth-dweller will trouble them again.*

To remain on the perch the Lord has established for me requires remaining stable and calm. There is a place the Lord has called each of us to and He has made a way for you to.

Hold steady... stay steady...

Stay: hold out, endure, pause, wait

> Steady: firmly place or fixed
> Stable in position or equilibrium
> Free from agitation; calm
> Firm; unfaltering [96]

Stay Steady

To endure to the end,
> To overcome various trials,
>> To persevere in the in-between places

Only God can steady us.
> Only His joy, His peaceful calm, enables us to get to the other side.

To remember the faithfulness of God in every season strengthens us.

---

[96] Dictionary.com

 *A Divine RE– The More Excellent Way*

> *We all experience times of testing, which is normal for every human being. But God will be faithful to you. He will screen and filter the severity, nature, and timing of every test or trial you face so that you can bear it. And each test is an opportunity to trust him more, for along with every trial God has provided for you a way of escape that will bring you out of it victoriously.[97]*

To remember Jesus revealed our Father's promise for help,

> *But when the Father sends the Spirit of Holiness, the One like me who sets you free, he will teach you all things in my name. And he will inspire you to remember every word that I've told you.[98]*

To remember to plant His word in our souls for this renews our minds and saves our souls.

> *So this is why we abandon everything morally impure and all forms of wicked conduct. Instead, with a sensitive spirit we absorb God's Word, which has been implanted within our nature, for the Word of Life has power to continually deliver us.[99]*

To remember we have the mind of Christ as human reasoning and unrighteous wisdom arises.

> *For we did not receive the spirit of this world system but the Spirit of God, so that we might come to understand and experience all that grace has lavished upon us. And we articulate these realities with the words imparted to us by the Spirit and not with the words taught by human wisdom. We join together Spirit-revealed truths with Spirit-revealed*

---

97 1 Corinthians 10:13 TPT
98 John 14:26 TPT
99 James 1:21 TPT

words. Someone living on an entirely human level rejects the revelations of God's Spirit, for they make no sense to him. He can't understand the revelations of the Spirit because they are only discovered by the illumination of the Spirit. Those who live in the Spirit are able to carefully evaluate all things, and they are subject to the scrutiny of no one but God. For

Who has ever intimately known the mind of the Lord Yahweh well enough to become his counselor?

Christ has, and we possess Christ's perceptions.[100]

To remember we have the helmet of Hope.

But since we belong to the day, we must stay alert and clearheaded by placing the breastplate of faith and love over our hearts, and a helmet of the hope of salvation over our thoughts.[101]

Embrace the power of salvation's full deliverance, like a helmet to protect your thoughts from lies. And take the mighty razor-sharp Spirit-sword of the spoken word of God. Pray passionately in the Spirit, as you constantly intercede with every form of prayer at all times. Pray the blessings of God upon all his believers.[102]

RE- Turn to the ancient path, in this New Day. Love what God loves, turn from what God hates and protect what is His by destroying the works of the enemy.

---

100 1 Corinthians 2:12-16 TPT
101 1 Thessalonians 5:8 TPT
102 Ephesians 6:17-18 TPT

My Reflections

47

SEE THREE

In November of 2020, I had a fall which caused serious injury and misalignment. I was knocked to the ground by my daughter's dog and my little dog. My neck was injured. I found out the C-3 was out of alignment and the nerves were inflamed. The nerve injury caused horrible jaw pain. It was difficult to sleep, eat, or drink much because of the pain.

The Lord reminded me of the prophet Bob Jones revelatory teaching on discernment. The revelation the Lord gave him when there is pain in the jaw was that it indicates emotions need to heal and align with God. We are not to be ruled by our emotions.

I prayed, repented, sought the Lord and also had to have some therapy for the injuries. The healing came when I began to see what the Lord was speaking to me about the season I was in. Literally being knocked off my feet by what could be interpreted a 'friendly mishap'. Those sweet dogs didn't mean to hurt me. Nor did my family and friends with their words regarding us re-locating again. (Ah another RE- word.)

My C-3 had to be RE-set in the physical, natural realm. In the spiritual it symbolizes my need for alignment and humility. The neck can represent a stiff-necked attitude. This can cause great pain and disruption.

I felt it is part of our needing to See Three, the Holy Three—Our Father, Jesus Christ his Son and Holy Spirit. It takes proper alignment to SEE Holy Three in their diverse attributes.

It is looking through the cross.
>   One with His death
>   Crucified with Christ
>   Resurrected with Christ
>   Ascended with Christ

When we are not looking through the cross, we become anxious and nervous.

In the In-Between
>   Focus on Him

In pain and suffering
>   Focus on Him

The Sunday of all Sundays is coming
Resurrection, healing life

C-3: See Three

Our alignment is with Christ.

> *But I will give all my thanks to you, Lord, for you make everything right in the end. I will sing my praise to the God of the Highest Place!*[103]

> *LORD, I will exalt you and lift you high, for you have lifted me up on high! Over all my boasting, gloating enemies, you made me triumph!*
> *Oh Lord, my healing God, I cried out for a miracle and you healed me!*[104]

---

103 Psalm 7:17 TPT
104 Psalm 30:1-2 TPT

The pain from this fall was horrific. I lost sleep. It was very challenging.
Many tears.

I cried out in anguished prayer: *Jesus, pray for me.*

When I prayed this, I began to see a turn-round.

Hebrews tells us Jesus intercedes for us.
His grace is released through His life.

> *So now, beloved ones, stand firm and secure. Live your lives with unshakeable confidence. We know that we prosper and excel in every season by serving the LORD, because we are assured that our union with the Lord makes our labor productive with fruit that endures.*[105]

SOZO Jesus re-set:
    Alignment
    Heart healing
    Spirit awakening
    Accountability to Holy Three[106]

Unstoppable
Christ's dominion

We get to partner with the Lord. As we get to know Him, we make Him known. To know Christ and Him crucified, making Him known through doing what He does.
To mend
To deliver from evil
To disciple

---

105 1 Corinthians 15:58 TPT
106 The Father, Son and Holy Spirit; Matthew 3:16,17, 28:19;

To HEAL: Heal, Encourage, Awaken, Love

The mature children of God are those who are moved by the impulses of the Holy Spirit. [107]

---

[107] Romans 8:14

48

BROKENNESS AND BEAUTY

My heart was crushed. My soul pierced. It affected my physical health as well. During my awakening to the Lord's Divine RE- He revealed to me I needed to understand what leaders go through. Would I trust Him in the process?

I awakened to the reality: *This is not just about me. This is about healing others.* I needed to surrender my heart to get to the place of full trust in God. Our callings are for His purpose. If we are self-centered, we will not be able to love the '*one another*'. This is because we can't see them through the lenses of self. We are reminded Omnivision is seeing through the Lord's lenses.

The Lord's lenses allow us to see the strongholds in people's lives. I struggled with this. I have prayed over and over to see after the spirit and not the flesh. In processing this I heard my Love say, *How will you set them free if you don't see what has bound them?* This is not seeing after the flesh, but by Holy Spirit discernment. It is a gift of love from Our Father God.

When we are told to only see good, only speak good…this is false light. Evil is evil, good is good. Jesus addressed the evil in lives with love and truth. His truth sets us free. Truth is love.

Getting my eyes off myself and on to the Lord brought deep healing. The Divine RE- process has opened my eyes to the calling of the harvest. Over and over the past 20+ years I have written about the harvest. My favorite place has been going to the dark and forgotten places to share the love of God.

Love is not real if it is not willing to bleed. Jesus bled. He bled in the garden, He bled when they put those piercing thorns of a crown on His beautiful head, He bled when they nailed His hands and feet to the cross, and He bled when His side was pierced—blood and water poured forth—He birthed us through His blood and water.

Love bleeds. Birthing happens with blood and water. His blood is holy. His living water gushed forth. We need to be cleansed and born again through His blood and water. His Spirit does this in us when we surrender to Him.

Jesus' blood gushed forth. His blood is Holy, His life flow of Living water gushed forth. A fountain of grace and healing was opened. A fountain of cleansing invites us to call upon Jesus: *Cleanse me in Your Blood, Lord Jesus. Wash me in Your living waters. Sprinkle Your blood over all my life and everything concerning me! Wash me in Your living waters. Sprinkle Your blood over all my life and everything concerning me!* He suffered and bled for us that we might live free. He was wounded with the most excruciating form of abuse and torment to establish us in His Kingdom.

Will we suffer and bleed with Him to display His love? Will we choose to step into Him through His blood and suffering to know His glory? Here the invitation in this Divine RE- to come into the throne of grace through His wounds, His pierced side. His blood and glory overcame and overcomes all evil.

Sometimes when we choose love, we will bleed. Life hurts at times. We can choose to believe we didn't do anything, but if we're honest, we know Jesus is the only one without fault or sin. In the process, we must recognize our faults and weaknesses. We all need a savior. When we begin to really live with Christ, abiding in Him, He appears in us and through us. Then others will look at us and say, "What must I do to be saved?". Pride just doesn't repel God, it repels the 'one anothers' we are called to.

Brokenness and beauty come from humility. Brokenness and humility are keys to our breaking through the hardness of hearts.

As we cry out to Jesus, *Wash me in Your living waters, cleanse me with Your blood, anoint me and all my life with Your oil of glory*…this is where divine access to all the help we need in every season is made available to us.

If we are to birth anything real and lasting, there will be tears and blood. What we birth we are called to nurture, help it grow and move forward.

This is all about the unexpected, the hidden…

    No agenda but Our Father's.

It's the becoming for others forming
Transformation
Overcoming.

Becoming who we are created to be so we can partner with the Master Potter in the forming of the 'one anothers'.

Trusting
  Believing
    Receiving

Going where He says go, giving what He gives, pouring forth from the abundance of Christ Jesus.

A Divine RE– The More Excellent Way

My Reflections

49

BROKEN AND POURED OUT

A personal life parable unveils a beautiful picture of brokenness.

Randy and I were staying in a hotel during our transition back from California to Utah. He was out with the dog. I wanted to prepare communion. In doing so, I dropped an entire bottle of grape juice on the tile floor. It shattered and all the contents spilled out.

To me it spoke of many of us who feel we have been dropped. Or perhaps life has had you fall on you face, kneeling in brokenness before Yeshua, pouring out all your life substance.

This bottle was broken at the doorway of our small hotel room. Broken, poured out at the doorway. I knew there was a simple revelation to apprehend. My husband knocked on the door to come back in, but it was a mess and I wanted to clean it first. I asked him to wait. Then I realized I needed his help.

He came in, saw what was needed and went to get cleaning supplies for the room. He asked me to sit with our puppy and hold her still while he cleaned up the mess. As I looked at him cleaning up the mess, I pondered, *This is what love looks like.* I was undone by this picture of love.

You see, our dog's name is Shiloh. Shiloh means "peace" and "tranquil."

My husband had me sit with Shiloh, in a posture of peace and tranquility while he took care of cleaning up the broken pieces. The fragrance of the grapes filled the room. Love's fragrance filled our hearts.

Psalm 31:12 tells how David felt in the midst of his broken mess:

> *I am forgotten as a dead man, out of mind;*
> *I am like a broken vessel.*

Yet by verse 22-24 he is crying out to God and giving praise to the one who his hope is in.

> *As for me, I said in my alarm,*
> *"I am cut off from before Your eyes";*
> *Nevertheless You heard the voice of my supplications*
> *When I cried to You.*
>
> *O love the Lord, all you His godly ones!*
> *The Lord preserves the faithful*
> *And fully recompenses the proud doer.*
>
> *Be strong and let your heart take courage,*
> *All you who hope in the Lord.*[108]

Perhaps David's discovery on his journey led him to realize brokenness was the place where he discovered all his hope was in the Lord. David had the ability to see the Lord in every season. Brokenness leads to tender reliance on the Lord. Relying on Him is where our strength is found. In every season may we discover all our hope is found in the Lord.

---

[108] Psalm 31 NASB

David's Consecration

Let my passion for life be restored,
tasting joy in every breakthrough you bring to me.
Hold me close to you with a willing spirit
that obeys whatever you say.
Then I can show other guilty ones
how loving and merciful you are.
They will find their way back home to you,
knowing that you will forgive them.
O God, my saving God,
deliver me fully from every sin,
even the sin that brought bloodguilt
Then my heart will once again be thrilled to sing
the passionate songs of joy and deliverance!
Lord God, unlock my heart, unlock my lips,
and I will overcome with my joyous praise!
For the source of your pleasure is not in my performance
or the sacrifices I might offer to you.
The fountain of your pleasure is found
in the sacrifice of my shattered heart before you.
You will not despise my tenderness.[109]

David's consecration in brokenness kept him pliable in the Lord's hands of purpose. When we consecrate our broken lives to the Lord, His heart receives us fully. We are the alabaster vessel being poured out for His divine purpose.

Brokenness and humility are the keys to breakthrough. These keys are needed for the harvest we are being released to bring into the fold. We had to go through some tough things to become pliable and soft in the Master's hands.

---

[109] Psalm 51:12-17 TPT

This is where His glory shines through our brokenness. The fragrance of His love poured out. The sound of hope is released when we surrender all for the One who sends us to one lost pearl He is searching for.

50

POOLS OF BETHESDA

Do you wish to be well?

The Healing at Bethesda

From Galilee, Jesus returned to Jerusalem to observe one of the Jewish feasts. Inside the city, near the Sheep Gate, there is a pool called in Aramaic, The House of Loving Kindness, surrounded by five covered porches. Hundreds of sick people were lying under the covered porches—the paralyzed, the blind, and the crippled—all of them waiting for their healing. For an angel of God periodically descended into the pool to stir the waters, and the first one who stepped into the pool after the waters swirled would instantly be healed.

Among the many sick people lying there was a man who had been disabled for thirty-eight years. When Jesus saw him lying there, he knew that the man had been crippled for a long time. Jesus said to him, "Do you truly long to be well?"

The sick man answered, "Sir, there's no way I can get healed, for I have no one to lower me into the water when the angel comes. As soon as I try to crawl to the edge of the pool, someone else jumps in ahead of me."

> Jesus said to him, "Stand up! Pick up your sleeping mat and you will walk!" Immediately he stood up—he was healed! So he rolled up his mat and walked again! Now Jesus worked this miracle on the Sabbath. [110]

When Jesus says to him, "Do you truly long to be well?" the translator notes in this interpretation:

> Or "Are you convinced that you are already made whole?" The Greek phrase *genesthai* is actually not a future tense ("want to be healed") but an aorist middle infinitive that indicates something already accomplished. Jesus is asking the crippled man if he is ready to abandon how he sees himself and now receive the faith for his healing. [111]

Pools of Bethesda mean: "House of Loving-Kindness."

We understand the Lord's glory is His loving-kindness when He reveals His glory to Moses in His encounter with him. [112]

When Jesus asks the lame man, "Do you long to be well?" He is asking him if he is ready to abandon how he sees himself and now receive faith for his healing.

Is this man ready to leave man-made pools and the idol of victim status? Is he ready to be RE-Created?

When Jesus appears to His disciples after His resurrection, he says to them, "Peace be with you." He is saying to them 'wholeness' be with you. He breathes upon them, His very breath. His RE-creation breath.

---

110 Matthew 5:1-9 TPT
111 Verse 6 Footnote TPT
112 Exodus 33:17-19

There are many in this season who see themselves through wounds and failures instead of being one with Jesus in His life, healing, and resurrection. The lenses of 'failure' open the door to a victim mindset. We are not victims when we step into life in Christ. We are overcomers in the glorious life of Jesus Christ.

> *The confidence of my calling enables me to overcome difficulty without shame, for I have an intimate revelation of this God. And my faith in Him convinces me that He is more than able to keep all that I've place in His hands safe and secure until the fullness of His appearing.* [113]

Our true calling is to be whole, fully alive sons and daughters. The Way Maker has made a way for us to live the overcomer's life.

> *For whatever is born of God overcomes the world; and this is the victory that overcomes—our faith. Who is the one who overcomes the world, but he who believe that Jesus is the Son of God.* [114]

To overcome is to conquer. Jesus conquered shame, sickness, disease, identity theft, death and every scheme of darkness. When we believe He is the Son of God, we are overcomers! Overcomers have something to overcome. It is part of our journey. Process leads through the valley of despair to the promise.

Many feel hopeless and I hear their echoes of despair:

> How can it be?
> I'm so broken
> I'm crushed

---

113 2 Timothy 1:12 TPT
114 1 John 5:4-5 NASB

> This isolation has crushed me.
> I'm angry
> I feel like a failure
> I feel I've fallen away.
> How do I move forward?

Jesus promised:

> *And everything I've taught you is so that the peace which is in Me will be in you and will give your great confidence as you rest in me. For in this unbelieving world, you will experience trouble and sorrows, but you must be courageous for I have conquered the world!"*[115]

Once again, to overcome is to conquer.

It is time to RE- member we are in a battle. This is a battle between Truth and deception, Light and darkness. It is a serious battle for the souls of man. We are awakening to the love-warrior mindset. Love conquers all, and the way love does this was revealed in every word, step, and action Jesus took. His whole life RE-vealed Our Father, who is Love.

> *Overcome every form of evil as a victorious soldier of Jesus the Anointed One.* [116]

Knowing the promises of the Promise Keeper will enable us to stand firm, pressing on with joy until the end. I have included many of these life-word promises intentionally. For it is the word of truth implanted in our hearts, which has power to deliver us from evil.[117]

---

115 John 16:33 TPT
116 2 Timothy 2:3 TPT
117 See James 1:21

But that's not all! Even in times of trouble we have a joyful confidence, knowing that our pressures will develop in us patient endurance.[118]

Seasons of trials strengthen us for the long and narrow road. Endurance is needed for the overcomer. There is a reward we are pressing towards.

And then as your endurance grows even stronger, it will release perfection into every part of your being until there is nothing missing and nothing lacking.[119]

Those who overcome are the conquering ones. We have the Overcomer living inside of us. Our hope is in Christ Jesus. Many lies have polluted the river of God in churches. Part of our overcoming is knowing the Truth. Jesus is the Way, the Truth and the Life. Jesus is enough.

Little children, you can be certain that you belong to God and have conquered them, for the One who is living in you is far greater than the one who is in the world.[120]

His grace leads us to His "House of Loving-Kindness," for He has made a way for us to live in wholeness.

Do you wish to be well?

---

[118] Romans 5:3 TPT
[119] James 1:4 TPT
[120] 1 John 4:4 TPT

A Divine RE– The More Excellent Way

My Reflections

51

STAND

In His presence receive His counsel and judgments for you. It is also here that He will give you His word against the enemy.

Stand and declare the word of the LORD!

Decree His Word.

When His word comes from His presence, it is His authorized word founded upon His holy written Word.

It is our covenantal position through the blood of Jesus Christ in God we stand in.

> STAND
>
> **S**trengthened
> **T**hrough
> **A**nointing
> **N**ow
> **D**ecree

Strengthened in the power of His might.

Through His presence you will pass through.

Anointed with TNT, you will NOW decree His Word![121]

---

121 TNT: Total Nucleus Transformation, power of Holy Spirit

STAND

Strengthened
Through
Anointing
Now
Decree

But the one who endures to the end, he will be saved.[122]

---

[122] Matthew 24:13 NASB

52

PIONEER

Pioneer:

The one who discovers
Who digs
Who plants
Who inspires
Begins building, but often does not settle into what is built.

A nugget the Lord shared with me is the fruit that comes from the hard work sown into pioneering a region is in the pioneer's eternal account. We are not to look at life through narrow lenses. We are to see with Father's eyes of faith.

We must learn to trust the Lord on the unknown path. Each revelation and every piece of the puzzle will help to strengthen the whole. We may not see the big picture when looking at our piece, but God sees the finish. Our little part blesses the body. We are invited to obey and do our little part, no matter the scale.

Pioneer:

You may have dug the well or re-dug a well.

You may have seen the first signs of hope as water gushed forth and oil began to flow.

 *A Divine RE- The More Excellent Way*

But when your part was finished, you were called to move forward to your next place.

Don't despair when those who took your place see more than you have ever seen.

Rejoice in the increased blessings being poured out on the multitudes.

Remember, if you hadn't put your hand to the plow, digging ditches through your tears, what is happening may never had.

So, rejoice and rest

As you Re-set.

As trauma bonds fall away and wounds are healed; scars become stars.

Transition peace.

Remain steadfast and faithful.

Don't measure success by who gets to pick the fruit.

Remember the vision.

The eyes of faith given to you to see.

The ears of trust, pierced, you've learned to obey.

Seeds sown and watered.

And when it's time again,

You will see the next,

You will hear the voice behind

As another adventure begins.

Re-member to trust—to lean on Him—to obey.

53

SETTLE–ABSOLUTELY NOT!

The Heart of a Pioneer

"Religion settles, revelation humbles."

Corey Russel

When our upheaval move happened, many would ask me if I was settled.

I would cringe at these words. My response strong: I am not settling. One day I asked the Lord for His wisdom regarding our move, as I was beginning to understand the eternal implications of A Divine RE-.

He gave me the word "Established." To be established in communion with Christ.

A Divine RE- The More Excellent Way

My Reflections

54

ESTABLISHED TO FLOURISH

Being rooted and grounded in Him is being established and steady in every season. It is discovering the process produces endurance and a flourishing life.

Ephesians 3:14-16

So, I kneel humbly in awe before the Father of our Lord Jesus, the Messiah,

the perfect Father of every father and child in heaven and on the earth.

And I pray that he would unveil within you the unlimited riches of his glory and favor until supernatural strength floods your innermost being with his divine might and explosive power.

Then, by constantly using your faith, the life of Christ will be released deep inside you, and the resting place of his love will become the very source and root of your life.

Then you will be empowered to discover what every holy one experiences—the great magnitude of the astonishing love of Christ in all its dimensions. How deeply intimate and far-reaching is his love! How enduring and inclusive it is! Endless love beyond measurement that transcends our understanding—this extravagant love pours into you until you are filled to overflowing with the fullness of God!

Never doubt God's mighty power to work in you and accomplish all this. He will achieve infinitely more than your greatest request, your most unbelievable dream, and exceed your wildest imagination! He will outdo them all, for his miraculous power constantly energizes you. [123]

One of the fruits of endurance is we are strengthened. In verse 16 the word *strengthen* is the Greek word *Krateioo* and it means:

- To prevail by God's dominating strength, i.e. His strength prevails over opposition
- For the believer (to attain mastery, the upper hand)
- Operates by the Lord in-working faith
- Strengthens you with power—Dunamis

Another fruit of endurance is we become rooted and grounded in Love. God is Love.

Verse 17 gives us the Greek word for rooted, which means:

- Take root, plant, fix firmly, establish

The Greek word for grounded means:

- Found, lay the foundation
- Establish, established

The Greek word for comprehend:

- May have power, full strength

---

123 Ephesians 3:14-16

Verse 19 segues us into the transcendent transformation power of Ruach Ha'Kadesh.[124]

Through the power of Holy Spirit, we will move into:

- Apprehending—knowing the full dimensions of the Lord
- Know the love of Christ that surpasses

Surpasses: transcends

  o Excels, exceeds

- Knowledge

  o Doctrine

  o Wisdom

- You may be filled: to fill—to complete
- With all the fullness, which means: fullness, sum total, even super abundance, supply—completion

When I received fresh revelation and understanding of these verses, I was undone. I felt compelled to keep reading and reflecting upon it. I had to savor the richness of the promises in this passage. The depth of the meaning of the words strengthened and undergirded me.

My paraphrase from this passage:

> We are established, and God's dominating strength prevails over every opposition. As a believer in Christ, I have the upper hand and am strengthened with power. I operate in the Lord's in-working faith.

---

124 Hebrew for Holy Spirit

He gives me endurance as I am established in His love. I am firmly fixed on His foundation. I am established and have full strength in the transcendent transformation power of Ruach Ha'Kadesh.

I am apprehending the full dimensions of the knowledge of the Lord. He is giving me His wisdom and filling me.

I am complete in Christ, super-abundantly supplied with His fullness.

Everything we need in every season is found in the fullness of Christ. Our Father sent His Son who made a way for the Promise of the Father to come. Holy Spirit, Our Father's promise, fills us, clothes us, and endues us with the Dunamis of Heaven. This is the TNT of Holy Spirit, the dynamite power to live a morally excellent life.[125]

The Branch of the Lord

> *The cut-off stump of Jesse will sprout,*
> *and a fruitful Branch will grow from his roots:*
> *the Spirit of Yahweh will rest upon him,*
>> *the Spirit of Extraordinary Wisdom,*
>> *the Spirit of Perfect Understanding*
>> *the Spirit of Wise Strategy,*
>> *the Spirit of Mighty Power,*
>> *the Spirit of Revelation,*
>> *and the Spirit of the Fear of Yahweh.*
> *He will find his delight in living*
>> *by the Spirit of the Fear of the Lord.*

---

125 TNT: Total Nucleolus Transformation

He will neither judge by appearances
nor make his decisions based on rumors.
With righteousness he will uphold justice for the poor
and defend the lowly of the earth.
His words will be like a scepter of power
that conquers the world,
and with his breath he will slay the lawless one.
Righteousness will be his warrior's sash
and faithfulness his belt.[126]

---

126 Isaiah 11:1-5 TPT

A Divine RE– The More Excellent Way

My Reflections

55

DIVINE PURPOSE IN UPHEAVAL

Ezekiel 3:12- MSG

Then the Spirit picked me up. Behind me I heard a great commotion— "Blessed be the Glory of GOD in his Sanctuary!"—the wings of the living creatures beating against each other the whirling wheels, the rumble of a great earthquake.

The Spirit lifted me and took me away. I went bitterly and angrily. I didn't want to go. But GOD had me in his grip. I arrived among the exiles who lived near the Kebar River at Tel Aviv. I came to where they were living and sat there for seven days, appalled.

At the end of the seven days, I received this Message from GOD:

"Son of man, I've made you a watchman..."

Verse 13 speaks of a Divine Earthquake released through the activity of the Living Creatures. The wheels within the wheels, wherever they move, the Spirit of the Lord is about to move.

It seems when we wait, we will "see" more of what the Lord is doing. An earthquake is an upheaval. It can uproot and expose hidden foundational issues. Likewise, an upheaval can uproot and expose those things not rooted and grounded in Christ. He has purpose in upheaval.

When the Lord invited me to read Ezekiel in *The Message Bible*, I knew a revelation awaited me. When I read chapters 1-3, I wept tears of relief as I felt His love in His Message. I saw an invitation to encounter, His voice inviting me "to remember" the calling. We are in A 'Divine RE'- a corporate calling for His people to be reset.

I was undone when I read verse 14: *I went bitterly and angrily. I didn't want to go.*

I can truly say I am thankful I never let go of God, and He never let go of me as it continues in verse 15; *But God had me in his grip.*

Realizing God had me in His grip I asked him: *You aren't angry with me?*

His answer: "No I am not."

A wonderful sense of freedom filled my soul. In drawing close to the Lord in His Word, the in-between place loses its grip of fear. Faith and hope in the grip of Love replace it. *Weariness and grief will disappear.*[127]

> *Yahweh's ransomed ones will return with glee to Zion.*
> *They will enter with a song of rejoicing*
> *And be crowned with everlasting joy.*
> *Ecstatic joy will overwhelm them;*
> *Weariness and grief will disappear!*[128]

---

127 See Isaiah 35:10 TPT
128 Isaiah 35:10 TPT

When upheaval uproots things the Lord wants exposed, we need to let Him have what is not for this season. We need to let go of the old ways, thought patterns, habits and all that was uprooted to be.

Upheaval can be likened to the 'threshing floor'. The wind of the Spirit is blowing and carrying away the chaff. Wheat is what will remain in the prepared place.

A Divine RE- The More Excellent Way

My Reflections

56

GO THROUGH

December 29, 2020, I heard these words of liberating truth from the Voice of Love.

You had to go through the dark night of the soul.
To feel anguish of dreams dying.
The ache of hopeless, grey shadows in valley of despair.
To feel,
  To know,
    To comprehend how deep the scorpions sting has left the souls of others paralyzed.
To recognize the bitterness of wormwoods' spell.
To remember…
    You have the authority to trample on serpents and scorpions.
      You carry the antidote to venom's poison.
        Antidote of HOPE in Christ.
          His Blood.
          His Anointing.
          His Life.
          His Light.
          His glory shining bright.
   A balm of peace.
   A poured-out offering delivering from
      Dis-couragement

> Dis-dain
> Dis-illusionment
> Dis-appointment
> Des-pair

Then I heard as clear as a bell:

> "Get on your horse of victory and ride."

My Love had me look up what ride means: to rest upon, to be carried.

My Love then spoke to me; it is movement in rest. Victory rest… To move forward in victory rest.

The hopeful words continued. On December 31, 2020, I heard the Lord speak:

> I have been faithful to My word to you.
>
> I have led you,
>
> Healed you,
>
> Delivered you,
>
> Empowered you.
>
> I have made you ready.

> *For whatever is born of God overcomes the world; and this is the victory that has overcome the world—our faith.*[129]

---

129 1 John 5:4

January 2, 2021, I see the hands of Yahweh pulling back the brass curtain of clouds that have been over my life and ministry. I know this is not just for me, but also for others who choose to go through the process.

The heavens are open and there is a bright shining light beaming down upon me.

> I hear the Lord—
>> Enter My rest and live free.
>> Moving swiftly
>> Empowered by union and communion
>> Apart from Me you can do nothing.
>> In Me—In Christ—You can do all things I show you.
>
> As I reveal My heart to you—
>> Your rhythm and grace fully aligned with My heart and will:
>>> Move forward
>>> No more delays.
>
> This is the time of culmination of every word and promise I, Yahweh, have spoken over your life.
>
> All you need is available—
>> I Am for you…Covenant Love…Covenant Fulfillment

Prayer:

Our Father, the Great I Am, I come to You and lean into Your heart and will for my life. Jesus is my source of Life, His love my power. Love overcomes. Love never fails. I am Yours and You are mine. Jesus, You are the greater One inside of me. Thank You for Your Holy Spirit, the very same Spirit that raised Christ from the dead. Help me to walk with You in humility, filled with Your empowering grace all my days. Give me Your heart for those You send me to love. Empower me with Your love to do as Jesus said to do. To announce the forgiveness of sins, the Kingdom has come. Grant me Your power through Your Holy Spirit to heal, awaken, encourage, and love as I follow You and lead the 'one anothers' to you. In Jesus' Name, Amen.

Let this hope burst forth within you, releasing a continual joy. Don't give up in a time of trouble, but commune with God at all times. [130]

---

130 Romans 12:12 TPT

57

AWAKENED TO TRUTH

I heard my Love speak: "Pick up your pen". Whenever I have heard this, He is about to speak something to me to scribe. I obeyed and worshipped until I heard His words to scribe.

Obedience—it is love choosing to look in Love's Eyes, saying yes with full assurance of His goodness.

Obedience—it is the cruciform life. Taking up our daily cross—laying down our will to be pierced through with His will for us.

It is like ear piercing—His love pierces us, and His grace adorns us and marks us.

For Him it was nails piercing His flesh as He took every sin and darkness so we could live in His light.

His look of love to the one who cried out for mercy…His words of liberation; "Today you will be with Me in paradise".

Nothing said to the haters except the most powerful prayer:

"Father, forgive them, they know not what they do".

No condemning look.
No pointing finger.

Talk about disagreeing views and opinion.

 *A Divine RE– The More Excellent Way*

Talk about accusations, lies, and verdicts of hell attempting to keep the souls of man in bondage.

Talk about opposing circumstances to what looked like dead promises hanging on that cursed tree—the cross of shame.

Yet what was not known or seen—The Sunday Of All Sundays was coming.

        A True North Star
        THE Morning Star

Hope shook the hills and mountains.
It didn't look like Hope or what natural eyes see and perceive as Hope.
It didn't sound like HOPE.
The sound sent shockwaves as running and hiding feet slipped on shaky foundations.

The silent pause,
The sting of death
Graves unearthed
The walking dead who had hoped in times past
Who had believed
But did not see
Until NOW
When all eternity watched an era end
Waiting for the emerging epoch
An epic shift
A sea-change moment
A marker in history where even how time was recorded shifted from BC to AD
Before Christ
After Death

An appearing of promise fulfilled—
> Every stripe
> Every lash
> Every pierce
> Released in fury
> PURCHASED GRACE,
> RELEASED HOPE
> An epoch of Christ's church birthed

And now an era has ended
The daughter of God,
The enemy of God attempts to silence and kill

Yet, Christ is coming again
His Bride awakening
She was fashioned in His split-open side
The cleft of the Rock
Hidden in secret glory
Until the day
The next epoch began to appear
She, His Bride
> His ecclesia
>> His people

Warrior lovers
Overcomers
Awakened to TRUTH

A sleeping giant awakened to the knowledge
We occupy until He comes
We stand
> We believe

A Divine RE- The More Excellent Way

In Him we are one
The answer to His final prayer
His last supper as a man
As He revealed His communion
The bread of His body broken
The wine of His blood poured out
His covenant
        His promise
To remember Him
        To do often
Until we are joined—reunited once again

He has never failed to keep a promise
He's never lost a battle

He is coming with His harvest sickle
And He is coming with His sword

Yet remember, oh little ones empowered by His grace

We do not know
As they knew not
What this Sunday Of All Sundays shall be

So keep on loving
Keep on believing
Keep on trusting
Keep on fighting the good and faithful fight

And keep on standing on the Lord's side
Today—this day
Choose the path of life.[131]

---

131 January 27, 2021

58

MOVE FORWARD

My spirit gets agitated when someone says we need to move-on.

I SHOUT NO, for I hear the Lord saying,

> Move forward.

To move on is to walk away in disappointment.
To move on may take you in the wrong direction.
To move on is to stop contending.
When we don't understand, we want to move on.

To Move Forward is to keep one's hand on the plow, to water, to weed, to nurture the Vision, the Word, and Promises of God.
In this you will see a harvest.

The Israelites chose to move on and settle.

Caleb and Joshua moved forward in the Spirit of Faith. They kept their eyes on the Way Maker, the Promise Keeper. They stayed steady. They chose to wait on the Lord. The day came when they contended for the promise and apprehended it.

The Lord revealed to me that the pain of moving back caused me to want to move on. Moving on is what we do when we don't understand.

Moving on is what the disciples did when Jesus was crucified. They fled. They hid. When Jesus was resurrected, He released *wholeness* to them. The Sunday of All Sundays, John 20 became our Eternal North Star.

It is the Sunday of All Sundays.

Faith does not need to understand. Faith thrives on TRUST.

To move forward is to step into yes with God and His call.
To move forward is to resist being ruled by emotions.
To move forward is to resist the devil. Darkness feeds on lies. Beelzebub sends his flies of lies to irritate.
To move forward is to advance—to move obstacles out of the way.
We move forward with the Spirit of Truth.
We move forward with heaven's marching orders.
Moving forward creates faith momentum.

The in-between place, as we transition from one era into the emerging Epoch, has two sides. Yes, I am saying sides. Each is fighting for our allegiance.

Darkness verses Light. Hell verses Heaven. Satan warring against Yahweh.

To move forward resist the darkness of hell.

May we recognize the time of our Divine RE-

The evil ruler of this world has his evil re-set. An agenda we are to RE-sist.

The enemy's unholy re-set is filled with:

>re-sentment
>re-bellion, pride

re-sisting God's will
re-sisting God's original intent and purpose

The sound of old tapes re-winding and failures being played out attempt to keep souls captive.

God re-writes our story when we become Born-Again. He Re-creates us in Christ.

> *For we are God's [own] handiwork (His workmanship), <u>recre-ated</u> in Christ Jesus, [<u>born anew</u>] that we may do those good works which God predestined (planned beforehand) for us [taking paths which He prepared ahead of time], that we should walk in them [living the good life which He prearranged and made ready for us to live].[132]*

Run to the Light
Let God's laser healing light RE-New your vision.

Some things died in the transition.
A seed that dies with God's promise in it will bear fruit again.
Some things need to be let go and remain dead and buried.

We don't need the tares in our souls to rise again.
We don't want the curse of hell to rise again in our lives.
We don't want the flesh to rise again.

> *I have been crucified with Christ; and it is no longer I who live, but Christ lives in me; and the life which I now live in the flesh I live by faith in the Son of God, who loved me and gave Himself up for me.[133]*

---

132 Ephesians 2:10 AMPC
133 Galatians 2:20 NASB

 *A Divine RE- The More Excellent Way*

It's Time to RE- Claim our position in Christ.
It's time for the RE- Generation to arise in RE-newed Life.
The same power that raised Christ from the dead…
    Honor the blood.
Receive glory resurrection power over your mind, will and emotions, over your body and every cell.
Your spirit RE-Aligned in Holy Three
Living in communion and union one with our Father, Jesus Christ, and Holy Spirit.

> *Keep in mind that we who belong to Jesus Christ have already experienced crucifixion. For everything connected with our self-life was put to death on the cross and crucified with Messiah. If the Spirit is the source of our life, we must also allow the Spirit to direct every aspect of our lives. So may we never be arrogant, or look down on another, for each of us is an original. We must forsake all jealousy that diminishes the value of others.* [134]

To move forward in A Divine RE- is to live in re-created life filled with Holy Spirit.

---

[134] Galatians 5:24-26 TPT

Our Father
I desire to seek You and know You in fasting and feasting.
In every season
With Your purpose and reason
To see You face to face
To know You heart to heart

You did not have me take off in the fog and shadows
You brought me to the Light of significance and clarity.
Vision to see—
Ability to hear—
Humility to align
Faithfulness to obey

  All in Christ
  In Christ
  One with Him
  His strength made perfect in my weakness
  Completing me in Him

His fullness and completeness
Empowering and enabling me to overcome
And fulfill every prophetic word.

And to help others experience
  Faith,
      Hope,
           Love,
To overcome
     To live in their fullness of purpose.
     Now Is The Time.
     Move Forward!

My Reflections

59

THE RE-GENERATION

And no one puts new wine into old wineskins; if he does, the wine will burst the skins, and the wine is lost and the bottles destroyed; but new wine is to be put in new (fresh) wineskins.[135]

You cannot repaint the old wine skin to make it new.
You cannot re-brand it for it to be new.
New wine needs a new wine skin…
A RE- New wine skin.

The Born-again life is RE-newal.
Awakening is RE-membering Who God is.

We are arising in resurrection.
It is time to come out of caves, up out of graves.
The blood of Christ RE-generates
We are the RE-Generation,
    I heard this resonating clear.

RE- has a powerful ability to shift. For the sake of understanding the revelation of *A Divine Re*, this is what the Lord highlighted in regard to the meaning of RE:

---

[135] Mark 2:22 AMPC

To depend on
To rest on
Respecting
Regarding

Generation means:
> period, generation, habitation, dwelling
> dwelling place

The Re-Generation: God resting upon a people who become His habitation.

> We RE-generate in the power of God.

RE-generate
> A generator releases power when the power goes out.

There is a RE-generation releasing the power of God even when others let the power go out in churches and gatherings across the nations.

> His RE-New Epoch,
> From era to Epoch.

His church age behind us, His Ecclesia RE-born, Awakened to purpose.

His Kingdom come,
His will be done.

Jesus' followers asked Him to teach us how to pray. Therefore we have "The Lord's Prayer". (See Matthew 6:9-13) This prayer has been released by multitudes over years.

 Now we see His Kingdom emerging…manifesting.

The Lord had me look at the spiritual difference between resuscitate and resurrection.

Resuscitate is to revive from apparent death or from unconsciousness.
Resuscitate is something man can do.

Resurrection Power is:

>A supernatural power released through the Spirit Breath Life of God.

Jesus was resurrected…not resuscitated.

In both instances there is death.

We are not promised a resuscitated life, where the old dead man is brought back.
We are promised a resurrection life in Jesus Christ…

>Being transformed
>Awakened
>Becoming fully alive
>>In His image, His likeness, His character.

Much of what has died in this season needs to remain dead.
Dying to self, the cruciform life. There must be death to live in resurrection life.

Jesus arose, no longer in a man's body of limitations.
He arose the crucified Lamb.
He took His eternal blood and put it on Heaven's altar.
Forever He made a way for all.
We are crucified in Christ
Old life dead
Risen in Him
NEW life

His Spirit
His Ruach
Breath of Life

A Divine RE- The More Excellent Way

Fully alive in Christ
No longer a flesh man
Oh, to apprehend this
A RE- Newed man
No longer a slave to sin

A RE- man (or woman)
A heavenly being
Born again by Ruach.

Do not resuscitate the dead.
Arise and live in the Born-Again Life
      Resurrection power
Release the RE-generation.

The Lord's process Re-veals purpose.
We are being prepared to be the people He rests upon.
We are the Re-generation, The generation of His habitation.

Jesus, Your blood was poured out. Your glory is being revealed. You paid the price for Your RE-Generation.

Those who go through process in this Divine RE- are the awakened RE-Generation.

Becoming alive with His resurrection breath!

The Gifts from this season are
Wisdom and Compassion.

60

POWER OF LOVE

The power of our Father's love will never go out. He is preparing a people for His glory:

        A Divine Re—

Transitioning from self-focus

    To God-centered focus.

        Willing to stand with Jesus—

            Willing that None Perish!

Transformers—those transformed into the image of Jesus Christ.
    Light bearers—Glory carriers

His Love Power will never go out as the Re-Generation bursts forth.

My Reflections

61

THE "IT IS FINISHED" POSTURE

What does *'yes'* look like?
    Surrender.
        Trust.
            Obedience.

It is hearing the words of Jesus, *"It Is Finished!"*[136]

It is seeing Jesus stand as HOPE right beside those who have been crushed by despair, disappointment, and doubt.

It is seeing Jesus say:
    Peace be with you.[137]

The Prince of Peace releasing peace. Peace is the essence of wholeness.

It is to know His yes has accomplished the will of Our Father, and He will accomplish in us and through us ALL He desires.

We yield with a steadfast *'Yes'*.
Surrendering with our *'Yes'*.
Trusting with our *'Yes'*.
Obeying with our *'Yes'*.

---

[136] John 19:29
[137] John 20:19-21

The "It Is Finished" Posture

NO FEAR.

Absolute Trust.

It is complete abiding.
No more hiding from destiny.

The only hiding
      Hidden in Christ,
          In the Rock,
              In His split open side.

Seated right beside
      Secure.
         Safe.
            Sheltered.
               Stable.

Holding onto Hope
The anchor of our soul,
Staying steady in every storm.

Confident in every promise
Trusting our Father
As Holy Spirit leads us
      In Christ,
Into His overcoming outcome.

Living in Light,
Not afraid of the night.
Truly love has overcome.
The victory is sure.

A Lovelution of fiery,
Burning bright,
Blood-bought warriors.

This is how we know
    The Truth has made us free:
We live in holy peace
    Shar Shalom our Bright Morning Star.

Peace is with us,
Peace be with you.
Breathed new life,
Upon hearts
    Once dead to life,
Now dead to sin
    Alive in Christ.

Living clothed
    In the Promise
        Of our Father.

For His fullness
    Is our inheritance,
        And we are His.

A signet ring of authority,
    Crowned with loving-kindness,
        Pierced through with The Truth.
  "It Is Finished"
Love has won the day.
No lie can prosper
Where Truth dwells.
No sorrow remains
Where Hope bursts forth.
Let faith say
I am finished—
It is a new day.

To say 'I am finished' is to receive by faith the complete work of Christ.

A Divine RE– The More Excellent Way

My Reflections

63

RE- BOOT

The Son shines into the fog of transition. Piece by piece a puzzle comes together. The picture appears, clarity comes, and we see what was hidden. Joy bursts forth with vision.

As I was going through the writings for this book, I had a divine appointment with RE- store, or restoration. The afternoon of April 24, 2021, I began to feel a presence upon the top of my head. It was a fluttering, like a gentle touch upon the crown of my head. This gentle presence manifested on and off all afternoon into the evening session of the gathering I was attending. I kept asking the Lord what was happening. I knew He would answer.

In the evening session, Chris Reed began to share a message: "Let No Man Take Your Crown." As he spoke, I was taken back into an encounter I had January 15, 2015. In this encounter. I awoke to the Lord speaking over me: A Crown, A King, And A Signet Ring. (I have included this message at the end of this section.) In this place of hearing a message, being in the presence of the Lord, I was in the encounter again. I felt the crown being Re-stored to my head. I wept tears of hope and joy as the Lord brought me into the restoration the crown of my calling. It was deep unto deep. The crown of rejoicing and overcoming was restored.

The night before, Chris had called out the angel of the Lord standing between me and another woman at the table. Angels on assignment Re-storing what the enemy had tried to re-move.

Chris shared the scripture from Revelation 3:11:

> *I am coming quickly; hold firmly to what you have, so that no one will take your crown.*

And 1 Thessalonians 2:19:

> *For who is our hope or joy or crown of exultation? Is it not even you, in the presence of our Lord Jesus at His coming?*

I was RE-awakened to the message of hope imparted to me in 2015. As I pondered this happening on my way home, I wrote what I heard from my Love. I have also included the revelation from 2015, as it is a NOW word, an eternal word.

A Crown,
    A King,
        A signet ring!

Overcoming grace
  Righteous authority
    Favor of the Lamb

Live from this place of grace
Overcoming every battle by the blood
Overcoming every trial by testimony and praise
Overcoming every test by dying daily

Take up your cross
Come follow Me

It's a different way
It's the Dawn of a New Day

Come and see
What I reveal to perceive

Come forth with joy!

The garments of grief—
    Discard!

Washed and cleansed
    In crimson tide
    Waves of glory love

Freedom's banner
    Hope's canopy
    Fiery shamar
    All encompassing
        All around

Hope's helmet
    Turban of authority
    Crowned in loving-kindness.

After I wrote these words I heard the Lord speak:

    It is Now time to RE- boot! The Lord brought us into His Divine RE- to Reboot.

Reboot:

> to restart (a computer) by loading the operating system; boot again.
>
> to produce a distinctly new version of…
>
> to make a change in (something) in order to establish a new beginning…[138]

This is the mandate of our day. To find the ancient path and allow the Lord to RE- boot us into His application of His ways for this epoch.

---

138 Dictionary.com

64

A CROWN

In March 2020, it was announced a worldwide pandemic was upon us. It was the beginning of COVID_19, the Corona-virus. Corona means crown. On March 10, 2020, I penned these words, and as the day ended, He put a rainbow in the sky to confirm His word.

No one is putting a crown on me.

Only One King in my life—King Jesus—and He wears the victor crown.

Any crown in my life comes from overcoming with Jesus He crowns us with loving kindness. He is reminding me of the word He spoke into me in 2015.

I shared this word at the end of 2015 after preaching this message where He led me during 2015. Get ready to arise in the Lord's authority!

Here is that word. (Following pages)

A Crown, A King, and A Signet Ring

Tracee Anne Loosle

Many of God's kids have gone through an intense warfare season. Some have been wounded by sickness, others by betrayal or rejection, and many others through hardship and losses. The message in this Heart Word Encouragement is to not focus on what happened at the devil's hands, but rather on what the Lord is saying now to those who persevered, overcame, and did not throw in the towel.

I woke up January 5, 2015, hearing these words over and over:

A Crown, A King, and A Signet Ring

The Lord invited me to stay in my place of rest as He kept speaking these words over me::

A Crown, A King, and A Signet Ring

It was a powerful impartation into my heart and spirit as the words literally reverberated with the vibrations of our Father's voice. I could feel the words go deep into me. I can also say that as I have shared this message, I have seen His authority manifest in a higher level than what I knew before.

I would like to break down each word and the meaning the Lord gave to me. I hope you will allow the Voice of the Lord to speak this into you. (We will make a link to this spoken message available to you on our website).

Let's look at the crown.

Crown (*Prophets Dictionary*):

- Symbol of war triumphs

- Signifies the highest level of achievement

- Emblem of victory worn by athletes as a badge of honor and courage

- Crowns are symbols of rewards of service and accomplishment

- Insignias of power and authority

Jewels in a crown represent the wisdom, wealth and resources, and instruments the crowned one's dominion possesses.

Crowns are normally worn during ceremonial processions and at times of formal service such as: court, judgment, promotion, or a coronation.

Crowns in Bible imagery signify what the wearer has accomplished, conquered, and gained rule over.

> "And to the angel of the church in Philadelphia write: He who is holy, who is true, who has the key of David, who opens and no one will shut, and who shuts and no one opens, says this: 'I know your deeds. Behold, I have put before you an open door which no one can shut, because you have a little power, and have kept My word, and have not denied My name. 'Behold, I will cause those of the synagogue of Satan, who say that they are Jews and are not, but lie -I will make them come and bow down at your feet, and make them know that

I have loved you. 'Because you have kept the word of My perseverance, I also will keep you from the hour of testing, that hour which is about to come upon the whole world, to test those who dwell on the earth. 'I am coming quickly; hold fast what you have, so that no one will take your crown. 'He who overcomes, I will make him a pillar in the temple of My God, and he will not go out from it anymore; and I will write on him the name of My God, and the name of the city of My God, the new Jerusalem, which comes down out of heaven from My God, and My new name. 'He who has an ear, let him hear what the Spirit says to the churches.' (Revelation 3:7-13)

A crown for the church of Philadelphia…The church of Brotherly Love. This is the church that did not give up or give in. For those of you who did not give up or give in, hold on to your crown. *Love never fails. (*1 Cor. 13:8)

We read in Song of Solomon 7:5-7 (TPT):

Redeeming love crowns you as royalty, guiding you into the fullness of humility and surrender,
Even a King is held captive by your beauty! How delightful and pleasing you are to Me. As I count all your delights—
Love has become the greatest!
You stand in victory above the rest, stately and secure. As you share with Me Your vineyard of love.

We need to see every victory won as a crown for Jesus. Even if the victory is that we did not quit, this indeed is a huge victory of perseverance. The crowns we will place before Him reveal every battle won. All of this is for the Lamb of God to receive the reward for His suffering as the Moravians declared.

The key to remember for today is: your crown reveals all the authority, wisdom, power, and authority of our God and King. In the heavenly realm your spiritual place with the Lord, the crown He gives, states to every power and principality to whose Kingdom you belong. It speaks of His authority, all He is, and all He has backing you.

This crown also speaks of promotions coming to those who have persevered. Get ready to receive ALL authority in Christ Jesus!

I had a dream a few months after the Lord gave me this revelation. In the dream, a huge crown was coming down upon me, covering every part of me. My daughter was standing in front of me, and she said, "The Lord is crowning you with loving kindness". What a gift for us! I have felt this crown come upon me when I share this word. May you also receive the impartation.

When we look at the word "King", we also need to remember that we are kings and priests. (1 Peter 2:9 and Revelation 1:6)

King *(Prophets Dictionary):*

- Kings were to rule by divine authority and supernatural grace
- The power that set the king in office was presumed to be the source of all his wealth, health, wisdom and military strategy
- Means the embodiment and crown of a tribe

There is only One Exalted, One Powerful, One King over all.

> *Yes, God will make Himself visible in His own divine timing, for He is the Exalted God, **The Only Powerful One, the King over every king, and the Lord of power!***
> *(1 Timothy 6:15 TPT)*

Our King rules over all; He is victorious and has overcome!

> *"These will wage war against the Lamb, and the Lamb will overcome them, because He is Lord of lords and King of kings, and those who are with Him are the called and chosen and faithful." (Rev. 17:14 NASB)*

> *From His mouth comes a sharp sword, so that with it He may strike down the nations, and He will rule them with a rod of iron; and He treads the winepress of the fierce wrath of God, the Almighty. And on His robe and on His thigh He has a name written, "KING OF KINGS, AND LORD OF LORDS." (Rev. 19:15-16 NASB)*

Our authority comes from God, the King of ALL the universe. Jesus was given ALL authority and power and He has given this to us.

Our kingly anointing is walking and talking in this realm of authority. Many operate in power but do not understand authority. Demons shudder when someone comes in authority. When we know who we are in Christ and walk in the revelation of authority, we bring heaven's transforming power to earth. This is where powerful decrees and declarations released from heaven's realm into earth shift and change situations and outcomes.

There is a warning in the story of the Sons of Sceva in Acts 19:

> *Some Jews who went around driving out evil spirits tried to invoke the name of the Lord Jesus over those who were demon-possessed. They would say, "In the name of Jesus, whom Paul preaches, I command you to come out." Seven sons of Sceva, a Jewish chief priest, were doing this. [One day] the evil spirit answered them, "Jesus I know, and I know about Paul, but*

who are you?" Then the man who had the evil spirit jumped on them and overpowered them all. He gave them such a beating that they ran out of the house naked and bleeding. When this became known to the Jews and Greeks living in Ephesus, they were all seized with fear, and the name of the Lord Jesus was held in high honor. Many of those who believed now came and openly confessed their evil deeds.

Are you yoked with Jesus and His wisdom, humbly and fully submitted to God, resisting the devil and your own flesh? (See James 3 and 4) Or has humility been a garment shunned, instead choosing to walk arrogantly proud of self and seeking worldly pleasures? I have been shown many will not be able to stand in the days to come because of compromise. The enemy will have access to harm them severely unless humility is truly embraced.

Authority comes to the humble and broken. Brokenness is a gift. Our weaknesses are gifts that cause us to know we need the One who is stronger to replace our weakness with His strength. It is a divine exchange. It is our covenant with Him.

Let us look at the ring.

Ring (Prophets Dictionary, in the Kings definition found):
For the marriage-like covenant between the regent and his or her God.

*Covenant (Prophets Dictionary):
agreement, accord or contract between two parties where the greater one forges a union that achieves a common goal that fortifies the lesser one's quality of existence. The spirit of covenant upgrades and enhances the lesser one's position in life.

Signet rings (ask.com; ehow.com):worn by highly decorated warriors as a sign of victory

Ancient kings used signet rings to designate authority, honor or ownership (gotquestions?.org)

God has made covenant with us. He gives us His signet ring. Look at the life of Joseph: he went through many trials, betrayals, being thrown into prison and forgotten. Yet the Creator of the universe had a plan to save a people during drought. God truly works all things together for good. Because Joseph embraced process, he came out receiving favor and authority, being given the king's signet ring.

> *Then Pharaoh took off his signet ring from his hand and put it on Joseph's hand, and clothed him in garments of fine linen and put the gold necklace around his neck. (Gen. 41:42 NASB)*

In Esther, we read a story of overcoming through being in the right place and surrendering to the Lord's will. In Esther 8, Mordecai is given the King's signet ring. He then writes a decree to be sent into the kingdom that overturns Haman's demonic decree that would have killed all the Jews. This decree is sealed with the King's signet ring of authority.

The Lord says we are His signet ring.

> *'On that day,' declares the LORD of hosts, 'I will take you, Zerubbabel, son of Shealtiel, My servant,' declares the LORD, 'and I will make you like a signet ring, for I have chosen you,' declares the LORD of hosts. (Haggai 2:23)*

Authority comes when we overcome…when we embrace suffering love with Christ Jesus, the Father will bring us through every trial and extend His scepter of favor granting us His signet ring of authority.

We carry His authority when we yield to His heart. When His heart resonates in ours, we become the voices that decree His will on earth.

Authority granted!

A Crown, A King, and A Signet Ring

Love, Grace & Glory,

Tracee Anne

To learn more about Tracee Anne Loosle,
visit her website: www.intrepidheart.org
Contact: admin@intrepidheart.org

Other books by Tracee Anne Loosle:
Heart of The Bride
Intrepid Warriors: Living a Life of Fearless Intercession
Vignettes from Heaven Volume 1; Revelation for Every Day

www.ingramcontent.com/pod-product-compliance
Lightning Source LLC
Chambersburg PA
CBHW070532090426
42735CB00013B/2960